CHARLIE H. CAMPBELL

One-Minute
Answers
to Skeptics

Concise Responses to the
Top 50 Objections
& Questions

Feedback on previous editions...

"I hope many seekers will give serious consideration to the thoughts so well expressed in this timely and pithy book. Well worth reading."
–Charles Colson

"This is a handy book with helpful answers for busy people."
–Norman Geisler

"A refreshing model of 'conversational apologetics!' This book will equip you to be 'always ready to give an answer for the hope that lies within you.'"
–Nancy DeMoss

"Here is a book that believers, especially new, growing Christians, should study and know well, perhaps even commit to memory!"
–The Baptist Bulletin Magazine

"Outstanding!...Such good answers!"
–Chuck Smith

"Christians are called to defend Christ, and this book gives great answers that will clear up a lot of confusion, both for the reader and for non-believers."
–ChristianBookPreviews.com

*For my Christian brothers and sisters
who desire to be better prepared to explain
why they are confident God exists and the
Bible is trustworthy.*

*Special thanks to Katie Armstrong
for her help editing the manuscript!
Email her at kmarmstrong88@me.com
for help editing your book.*

ONE MINUTE ANSWERS TO SKEPTICS
Concise Responses to the Top 50 Objections & Questions

Copyright © 2018 by Charles H. Campbell
Published by ABR—The Always Be Ready Apologetics Ministry
P.O. Box 130342, Carlsbad, CA 92013
Email: abr@alwaysbeready.com

Additional copies of this book can be found at **AlwaysBeReady.com.**

ISBN: 978-1721195213

Cover design and interior layout by the author.

Printed in the United States of America.

Contents

1. There's absolutely no evidence **God*** exists!

2. The **Bible** was written by men! It's not trustworthy.

3. Surely God doesn't exist. If He did, He'd **appear** to us in a public setting and prove it to the world.

4. I contend that you and I are both atheists. You don't believe in **Zeus** or Thor and neither do I. I just take it one deity further, I don't believe in your god either.

5. The Bible condones **slavery**! Only evil, selfish men would concoct a book like that!

6. The God of the Old Testament commanded **genocide**, the wiping out of the Canaanite people in the Book of Joshua. A loving God would never command such a thing!

* *Words in bold are keywords to help you quickly locate certain objections.*

7. The whole story about Jesus was plagiarized from ancient Egyptian myths about Horus! **Horus** was born on December 25 to a virgin. He was worshipped by three kings. He was a teacher by age twelve. He had twelve disciples. He was called "The Lamb of God." He was crucified, buried for three days, and then resurrected!

8. After the Roman Emperor **Constantine** became a Christian in AD 312, the Roman Empire took control of the Bible and tampered with its contents to better control the people.

9. You think Christianity is true because you live in the West and were brought up in the Christian faith. If you had been born in India, you'd be a **Hindu**!

10. With hundreds of **religions** in the world, it would be impossible to investigate all of them and know which one is true!

11. A loving God would never send people to **Hell**.

12. You Christians say the universe needs a maker because things don't just pop into existence from nothing. If that is the case, then God needs a **maker**! Who made God?

13. How can the Bible be true when it says the universe is only **6000 years** old?

14. The Biblical authors made several errors when they spoke about the natural world—I'll trust in **science** any day over your antiquated Bronze-Age collection of fables.

15. The universe is so **vast**! It's foolish to think a god built a universe billions of light years across just to have a personal relationship with you.

16. If God exists, why won't He just heal an **amputee** by restoring his limb? Then we would all know He exists!

17. **Evolution** is a proven fact. I stopped believing in your imaginary sky daddy a long time ago!

18. Religions, Christianity included, are responsible for most of the world's **wars**, suffering, and atrocities!

19. The Bible has been **tampered** with and changed so many times down through the centuries, we can't trust it today, even if it was once trustworthy.

20. The world is a mess! To think there is a loving God who allows all the evil and **suffering** that takes place is preposterous!

21. What about countries where hundreds of thousands of people are **starving**? What kind of God would create a planet that would put people through that kind of horrendous suffering? Certainly, not a loving one!

22. Only a cruel God would stand by and allow young innocent **babies** to die!

23. There's no evidence Jesus ever **existed**!

24. The New Testament authors stole the whole idea for Jesus's **virgin** birth from ancient religions like Mithraism.

25. Jesus's disciples made up the stories about His **miracles**.

26. There's no evidence Jesus rose from the **grave**!

27. It's outrageous to think God would only save people who have a **relationship** with Jesus!

28. Jesus's **earliest** followers never thought of Him as God!

29. The Gospels are full of **contradictions**!

30. The Gospels were written down **300 years** after Jesus lived!

31. The New Testament doesn't tell us the whole truth about Jesus. Christians purposely left other writings about Him out of the New Testament, for example, *The Gospel of Judas* and *The Gospel of **Thomas***.

32. It's ridiculous to think that all the races, with their different skin colors, came from **Noah's** family!

33. There are so many different **translations** of the Bible, no one could possibly know which one to trust!

34. You can't be sure of what the Bible means. Look at all the Christian **denominations**. Even they disagree about what to believe!

35. Churches are full of **hypocrites**!

36. Why do you Christians persist in **judging** people when Jesus said not to judge?

37. Why do Christians hate **homosexuals** and say they are going to Hell?

38. Belief in God is a **crutch**! Christians believe in God because they're weak and afraid of facing life and death on their own.

39. It's foolish to believe in things you **can't see**, like this God you speak of.

40. The Bible is oppressive and harmful to **women**!

41. We look at ancient Greeks, with their gods on a mountaintop, throwing lightning bolts, and say "They were so silly,

so primitive and naïve. Not like our religion. We have burning **bushes** talking to people, and guys walking on water. We're so sophisticated."

42. I believe in **science**! Most scientists are atheists. So, I find science and Christianity to be incompatible.

43. A talking **snake** in the Garden of Eden (Genesis 3)? How do you believe this stuff?

44. All religions basically teach the same thing. If a person is **sincere**, it's all going to be okay in the end.

45. Christians worship the same God as **Muslims**!

46. That's just your **interpretation** of the Bible!

47. I will never be happy in **Heaven** if my friends and family end up in Hell.

48. You should stop trying to **force** your beliefs on people!

49. I'm a **good** person. Surely, God is not going to send good people to Hell!

50. You Christians are so **narrow-minded**! Insisting that a person has to have a relationship with Jesus to go to Heaven is preposterous!

*"Always be ready to give a defense...yet
do it with gentleness and respect"*
–Peter (1 Peter 3:15)

Introduction

Have you ever tried to talk to someone about God or the Bible only to have your attempt shot out of the sky with an objection like:

- "There's no good evidence that God exists!"
- "The God of the Old Testament commanded the Israelites to commit genocide!"
- "The New Testament authors stole the idea for Jesus's life story from religions that were around long before Christianity!"
- "The Bible condones slavery, oppresses women, and promotes hatred of homosexuals!
- "Religions are responsible for most of the world's wars, suffering, and atrocities!"

Many critics of Christianity have an arsenal of these conversation-halting objections ready to unload at the slightest inkling a Christian is trying to talk to them about Jesus. Have you heard some of these? If you've tried to share the gospel with people in the twenty-first century, you have. Question for you. Did you feel prepared to "contend earnestly for the faith which was once for all delivered to the saints" (Jude 1:3)? Unfortunately, many Christians do not.

As an itinerant apologist, I regularly speak at different churches throughout North America, and almost every Sunday, people tell me:

- "I have heard these kinds of objections several times, but haven't known how they could be answered."
- "My coworker said _____ this week and it caught me completely off guard. I didn't know what to say."
- "I knew there was a solution to this dilemma, but I didn't know *what* it was, *where* to look for it, or *who* I could trust on the matter."
- "I've been a Christian for several years and have never heard a single sermon that addressed this tough topic in an in-depth fashion. We need more apologetics content on Sunday mornings!"

This kind of feedback week after week is one of the reasons I continue traveling, speaking, and writing. My desire is to help Christians stand strong in the truth, and be better equipped to answer atheists, skeptics, and people in false religions and cults.

In this updated edition of *One-Minute Answers to Skeptics* I answer what I think are the top 50 objections to God, the Bible, and Jesus.[1] As in the earlier editions of this book, I respond to the objections and questions in a conversational way. By that, I mean that I share the actual wording I might use in a conversation with a skeptic.

As the book title implies, the answers to each objection are intentionally concise. Obviously, much more could be said in response to every objection. But I am writing this book for busy people who don't have the time to go through my other books, videos, and articles, but who still want to be better prepared to respond to critics.

I pray that God will use this tiny book to:

- strengthen your relationship with Him
- fortify your confidence in the Bible
- inspire you to share the good news about Jesus
- equip you to "always be ready to give a defense" (1 Peter 3:15)

Grace and peace to you,

Charlie Campbell
Southern California, July 11, 2018

---

1. I'm not suggesting these are skeptics' *hardest* objections to answer or that there is survey data to back up an objection's inclusion in this book. The objections in this book are simply the ones I think skeptics raise most. They are also not laid out in any particular order. If there are objections you think I've overlooked that should make a top 50 list, share them with me at abr@alwaysbeready.com.

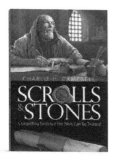

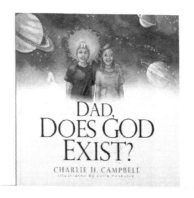

Scrolls & Stones

Do you know someone who struggles with trusting the Bible? Get him this book. Charlie lays out ten pools of evidence for the reliability of the Bible, including:

- fulfilled prophecies
- archaeological finds
- ancient writings that corroborate details in the Bible

Dad, Does God Exist?
(for ages 7–11)

After Sarah's faith is challenged by a classmate, she asks her dad, "What evidence is there that God exists?" His answer and interesting around-the-house analogies will help your child begin to grasp some of the reasons he or she can be *sure* the God of the Bible exists.

Available today at
AlwaysBeReady.com

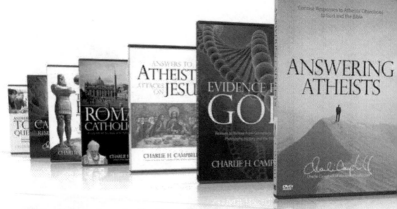

OWN ALL 34 OF CHARLIE CAMPBELL'S VIDEOS & AUDIO LECTURES ON THIS TINY USB FLASH DRIVE

Available at
AlwaysBeReady.com

1. "There's absolutely no evidence God exists!"

I find it interesting you've concluded that. Might I ask you a question? What are some of the supposed evidences you've rejected?[2] What books have you read wherein the author lays out what he thinks is evidence for God? I'm sure you've read some of them before concluding "There's absolutely no evidence God exists!"

I think there's compelling evidence for God. For example, consider the human body.[3] Your body has 206 bones,[4] about 700 muscles,[5] and a heart that beats over a 100,000 times a day as it pumps about 75 gallons of blood an hour through more

....
2. As with all the questions I ask the skeptic in this book, I would ask the question humbly and lovingly, and then allow the person time to respond.

3. Although there are several lines of evidence for God, I often like to start by pointing to the human body because this is an evidence for God that goes with the skeptic everywhere he goes.

4. Donald Rizzo, *Fundamentals of Anatomy and Physiology* (2016), 175.

5. Innerbody, "Muscular System," http://www.innerbody.com/image/musfov.html.

than 60,000 miles of veins, arteries, and capillaries.[6] The eyes you're looking through right now are composed of more than two million working parts.[7] Do you really believe all those muscles, bones, and organs pieced themselves together and started functioning apart from a designer?

What tells the cells and organs in your body how to function and what to do? It's the DNA inside the cells. The DNA in every one of your body's 37 trillion cells[8] contains a staggering amount of information. Where did this information come from? Bill Gates said DNA is like a computer program but far more advanced than any software Microsoft has ever created.[9] The British molecular biologist, Francis Crick, an atheist and one of the two scientists who discovered DNA, "estimates the odds that intelligent life exists on the Earth as the result of non-directed chance to be around 1 in 10 to the two billionth power."[10] Now of course you're free to believe life came about by non-directed, natural causes. I wouldn't bet against God's existence with such overwhelming odds. It would be far wiser to conclude that the incredible complexity we find in living organisms is the result of an intelligent designer—God.

....
6. Arkansas Heart Hospital, "Amazing Heart Facts," https://www.arheart.com/heart-health/amazing-heart-facts.

7. Eye Institute, "The Eye is One of the Most Complex Organisms in the Human Body," https://www.eyeinstitute.co.nz/About-eyes.

8. Rose Eveleth, *Smithsonian*, "There are 37.2 Trillion Cells in Your Body," October 24, 2013, https://www.smithsonianmag.com/smart-news/there-are-372-trillion-cells-in-your-body.

9. Bill Gates, *The Road Ahead* (1996), 228.

10. Mike Licona, "Answering Lenny Flank's Article Against Intelligent Design," https://www.risenjesus.com/answering-lenny-flanks-article-against-intelligent-design.

"We have only to see a few letters of the alphabet spelling our name in the sand to recognize at once the work of an intelligent agent. How much more likely, then is the existence of an intelligent Creator behind human DNA, the colossal biological database that contains no fewer than 3.5 billion "letters"—the longest "word" yet discovered?"

–John Lennox

2. "The Bible was written by men! It's not trustworthy."

Have you read the Bible? Have you read any books or articles that give good reasons to reject the Bible? Were those books or articles written by men? By your own reasoning, then, that would mean that what you've read is not trustworthy.

Just because something was written by men doesn't mean it's not trustworthy. Humans *are* capable of communicating the truth. Saying otherwise would undermine the trustworthiness of everything you say. So, humans can communicate truthfully. And what if those who desired to communicate truthfully even had God's *help* as they wrote—to ensure there were no errors? Then things would turn out really well, wouldn't they?

That is how the books of the Bible were written. God revealed Himself to certain people like Moses, Peter, and Paul, who wrote down what they saw and heard (Exodus 34:27; Jeremiah 30:2; 1 Timothy 3:16). And we believe there are several good reasons to trust what the authors of the Bible wrote.

The Bible, unlike any other ancient religious writing, has a wealth of evidence to support its reliability: hundreds of fulfilled prophecies, thousands of archaeological discoveries, its incredible internal harmony, historical confirmation in the ancient records of the Assyrians, Babylonians, and Romans, numerous scientific discoveries that have helped to validate different details in its pages, and so on. If I give you a book that lays out ten different lines of evidence for the Bible, would you be willing to read it?[11]

> *"I have a fundamental belief in the Bible as the Word of God, written by those who were inspired. I study the Bible daily."*
> –**Isaac Newton**

3. "Surely God doesn't exist. If He did, He'd appear to us in a public setting and prove it to the world."

You mean, like the time God came to the Earth in the person of Jesus, raised the dead, healed cripples, and opened the eyes of the blind, only to then be dragged away and nailed to a cross?

My friend, God has *already* appeared publicly to humans. God knows that appearing to you publicly won't change your heart. He knows that He's already provided enough evidence for His existence for those who truly want to know Him (Psalm 19:1–4; Romans 1:19–21; Acts 14:16–17).

You can freely choose to reject Him, but be assured of this:

---

11. I like to give away copies of my book, *Scrolls and Stones: Compelling Evidence the Bible Can Be Trusted* (2014), available at: bit.ly/stones-scrolls.

on the Day of Judgment when you stand before God, and your sins are exposed, saying "The evidence for God wasn't clear enough," is not going to work. Surely the evidence is clear enough.

> *"God has provided enough evidence in this life to convince anyone willing to believe, yet he has also left some ambiguity so as not to compel the unwilling. In this way, God gives us the opportunity to either love him or to reject him without violating our freedom."*
> **–Norman Geisler** and **Frank Turek**

> *"God maintains a delicate balance between keeping His existence sufficiently evident so people will know He's there and yet hiding His presence enough so that people who want to choose to ignore Him can do it. This way, their choice of destiny is really free."*
> **–J. P. Moreland**

4. "I contend that you and I are both atheists. You don't believe in Zeus or Thor and neither do I. I just take it one deity further, I don't believe in your god either."

Ah, it sounds like you're trying Richard Dawkins's "amusing strategy" in his book, *The God Delusion*.[12] Friend, look up the

----

12. Richard Dawkins, *The God Delusion* (2006), 53.

word *atheist* in any respected dictionary. An atheist is someone who doesn't believe in the existence of any god. I *do* believe God exists. So, I am not an atheist in the slightest degree.

Now, I understand why you don't believe in Zeus or Thor. There's no good evidence they exist, and there never was. That's why it's hard to find anyone today who believes in either of them. But more than two billion people believe in the God of the Bible, including well-educated scientists, doctors, philosophers, historians, and the like. Why do you think that is?

I think it's because there is good intellectually satisfying evidence for the God of the Bible. For example, there's the incredible fine-tuning of the universe, the mind-boggling complexity of living organisms, the information encoded into DNA. There's hundreds of fulfilled prophecies in the Bible. There's historical evidence for Jesus's life, death, and resurrection. Did you know that more than a hundred details about Jesus's life (as recorded in the New Testament) have been corroborated by historical sources *outside* the New Testament?[13] So, for these reasons and several more, many of us have concluded God exists.

If I were to share an article, book, or video with you that laid out some of these evidences for God, would you be willing to read or watch it?[14]

....

13. Gary Habermas, *The Historical Jesus: Ancient Evidence for the Life of Christ* (1996), 187–228, 243–255.

14. Evidence for God resources can be found here: AlwaysBeReady.com/god-evidence.

"I am persuaded that men think there is no God because they wish there were none. They find it hard to believe in God, and to go on in sin, so they try to get an easy conscience by denying his existence." –**Charles Spurgeon**

5. "The Bible condones slavery! Only evil, selfish men would concoct a book like that!"

Slavery was never part of God's original plan for humanity and it wouldn't exist if it weren't for humans living in rebellion to God's instructions. Friend, the Bible says to "love your neighbor as yourself" (Leviticus 19:18; Matthew 22:39) and to "regard one another as more important" than ourselves (Philippians 2:3). How could slavery flourish, if we all loved one another that way? A loving person doesn't kidnap people, lock them up, and force them to work. Kidnapping humans is a sin that carried the death penalty in the Old Testament (Exodus 21:16; Deuteronomy 24:7). And buying and selling slaves is condemned in the Bible alongside murder (1 Timothy 1:8–10).

Why then does the Bible have a handful of verses instructing people on how to treat slaves (Colossians 4:1)? Well, in Biblical times, people could *sell themselves* to be servants to pay off debts (Leviticus 25:39). And that was very common. So, for the servants' sakes, God gave the Israelites instructions regarding the treatment of servants. The instructions were given to *protect* and *help* the servants, not harm them or keep them down. For example, Exodus 20:10 said that servants were to have every seventh day of the week off. Deuteronomy 23:16 said to not mistreat a slave.

It was Christians who understood God's heart for kidnapped and mistreated slaves, who led the fight to abolish slavery in England and America long ago.[15] And Christians are at the forefront of the battle to eradicate the sex-slave trade today.[16]

6. "The God of the Old Testament commanded genocide, the wiping out of the Canaanite people in the Book of Joshua. A loving God would never command such a thing!"

Have you read the Old Testament passages regarding the Canaanites? What were the Canaanites doing that brought God's judgment on them? I'm interested to hear your take on it…Oh, you haven't read the passages? You forgot?

The Bible tells us the Canaanites at the time of Joshua were an exceedingly wicked people who were indulging in incest, adultery, polygamy, bestiality, witchcraft, child sacrifice to an idol named Molech, and a variety of other "abominable customs" (Leviticus 18; Deuteronomy 18:9-14). The Canaanites had become a dangerous threat to their posterity, neighbors, and the Israelites. So, God determined the Canaanites'

....
15. For more on this, see Alvin Schmidt's book *How Christianity Changed the World* (2004), especially the chapter "Slavery Abolished: A Christian Achievement," 272–291.

16. Ruth Graham, "How Sex Trafficking Became a Christian Cause Célèbre," March 5, 2015, http://www.slate.com/articles/double_x/faithbased/2015/03/christians_and_sex_trafficking_how_evangelicals_made_it_a_cause_celebre.html.

time on His planet was up.

God created the Earth and all its inhabitants, and He has the right to do whatever He deems best with His creation. All life belongs to Him.

Think back with me to World War II. Most of the world today believes the Allied Powers had the right to go to war against Japan and the Nazis to stop the great evils they were committing. If human governments have the right to send in a military force to put a stop to evildoers, doesn't God have the right? Surely, He does! If you had lived at the time of Joshua and were aware of the great atrocities going on in Canaan, you probably would have been in *favor* of God's intervention—unless you think burning children alive is okay.

7. "The whole story about Jesus was plagiarized from ancient Egyptian myths about Horus! Horus was born on December 25 to a virgin. He was worshipped by three kings. He was a teacher by age twelve. He had twelve disciples. He was called "The Lamb of God." He was crucified, buried for three days, and then resurrected!"

Have you done any real research on Horus? Or did you just watch a video on YouTube? *Zeitgeist*, the viral YouTube video that popularized this objection, is poorly-researched and brimming with errors and fabrications.[17] In fact, everything you just stated about Horus is false.

Horus, the ancient Egyptian falcon-headed sky god, was a mythological deity, not a real historical person like Jesus. So, it's hard to compare the two. But if you'll read an encyclopedia or dictionary on ancient religions, you'll quickly discover that Horus wasn't born to a virgin. The myths say he was conceived by his parents Isis and Osiris.[18] Nowhere do the myths say Horus was born on December 25. And even if he had been, the Bible nowhere tells us that Jesus was born on that date. The December 25 tradition originated long after the Gospels were written.[19] The Gospels' accounts of Jesus's birth don't mention three kings, only an undisclosed number of *magi* (Matthew 2:1), commonly known as wise men, not kings. Horus was never crucified. Crucifixion had not even been invented at the time *Zeitgeist* says the Horus myth originated, around 3000BC. Horus is not even reported to have died in most of the Egyptian myths. And Horus was never resurrected.[20] There's nothing about Horus becoming a teacher at age twelve. And there's nothing about him having twelve disciples.

Friend, there's no evidence Jesus's disciples stole any details for Jesus's life from mythological tales about Horus. Check out

....

17. *Zeitgeist*, https://www.youtube.com/watch?v=pTbIu8Zeqp0.

18. "Horus: Egyptian God," https://www.britannica.com/topic/Horus.

19. Andrew McGowan, "How December 25 Became Christmas," December 3, 2017, https://www.biblicalarchaeology.org/daily/biblical-topics/new-testament/how-december-25-became-christmas; John MacArthur, "Why do we celebrate Christmas on December 25?" https://www.gty.org/library/questions/QA68/why-do-we-celebrate-christmas-on-december-25.

20. "Horus," *Ancient History Encyclopedia*, https://www.ancient.eu/Horus.

the website AlwaysBeReady.com. Click on the "Zeitgeist" link. There are resources there by scholars and experts who refute the video point by point.

> *"Preach the word…For the time will come when they will not endure sound doctrine; but…will turn away their ears from the truth and will turn aside to myths."*
> –**Paul** (2 Timothy 4:2–4)

8. "After the Roman Emperor Constantine became a Christian in AD 312, the Roman Empire took control of the Bible and tampered with its contents to better control the people."

How did you come to that conclusion? Friend, there isn't a shred of evidence the Roman Empire tampered with the Bible. And the ancient handwritten manuscript copies of the Bible that *predate* the time of Constantine prove this to be the case. What do I mean? Well, we *know* what the Bible said *before* Constantine was even born, around AD 280. And when we compare the Bible we have and use today to those ancient manuscript copies of the Bible, we see that it says the same thing it said all the way back in the first, second, and third centuries.[21]

---

21. The Center for the Study of New Testament Manuscripts has hundreds of high quality photographs of ancient Biblical manuscripts on their website: csntm.org/About/WhoWeAre.

Would you be willing to read through the New Testament and familiarize yourself with Jesus's life and teachings? I'll happily give you a copy of the New Testament. I think you'll find Jesus to be incredibly interesting...and you may just fall in love with Him, as more than two billion of us have.

> *"When someone says to me, "Reincarnation was originally part of Christian teaching, but was taken out of the Bible in the fourth century," I always ask them to explain how that works...*
>
> *How does someone remove select lines of text from tens of thousands of handwritten documents that had been circulating around the Mediterranean region for over three hundred years? This would be like trying to secretly remove a paragraph from all the copies of yesterday's L.A. Times. It can't be done."*
> **–Greg Koukl**

9. "You think Christianity is true because you live in the West and were brought up in the Christian faith. If you had been born in India, you'd be a Hindu!"

So, you're assuming the only reason I'm a Christian is because my parents indoctrinated me? Interesting. I'm actually a Christian because I examined the evidence for God, carefully weighed the evidence for Jesus's life, death, and resurrection, and concluded it was reasonable to place my faith in Him. But might I ask you a couple questions?

Are you an atheist? Were your parents or college professors atheists? Might you then just be an atheist because of what they taught you? Should we discount atheism because of how you came to believe it? No. Accepting or rejecting an idea because of its source, rather than its merit, is to commit a "genetic fallacy." It's faulty reasoning.

So, even *if* a person is a Christian largely because of his parents' influence, that in no way undermines the truthfulness of Christianity. The Christian faith has flourished for two thousand years in large part because there are very good reasons to take it seriously. You might contact some of the 24 million plus Christians in India; they'd be happy to tell you why they are followers of Jesus.[22]

10. "With hundreds of religions in the world, it would be impossible to investigate all of them and know which one is true!"

Do you really want to know which one is true? Are you willing to investigate even one religion? Okay, good. Now, question for you. Do you drink coffee? When you sit down at your computer to buy a new coffee maker, not having any idea which brand or model to buy, what do you do? If you're like most of us, you start looking at user reviews, right? A coffee maker with 5,000 reviews and a 4.5-star rating, is going to be a pretty

22. This figure is based on 2001 census information provided by India's Office of the Registrar General & Census Commissioner, http://censusindia.gov.in/Census_And_You/religion.aspx.

solid product, right? Now, what if the store was running a Christmas special, and that top-rated, most-loved, coffee maker was free? Well! A person wouldn't need to waste time researching all the other coffee makers that have one or two-star ratings, right? He would order his free coffee maker.

So, here's what I propose. If you'd really like to figure out which religion is true, don't waste time researching the smaller religions. They haven't attracted many followers because the evidence for their truthfulness is not there. And there are a plethora of other reasons to reject them. Researching them would be like wasting time researching the coffee makers that have one and two-star ratings. Start with the religion that has attracted the most adherents (the one with the best reviews, so to speak), the one that has convinced more than 2 billion people it's true, and the only one that offers forgiveness of sins, peace with God, and everlasting life as a "free gift" (Romans 6:23)—Christianity.

Now, you might be wondering, "How do I investigate Christianity?" Here's what I suggest. First, go right to the primary sources. Read the four Gospels in the New Testament: Matthew, Mark, Luke, and John. These are accounts of Jesus's life and teachings that were written by His first followers.

Secondly, as you're reading, call out to God in prayer. Tell Him, "I want to know You! Reveal Yourself to me. Help me know if what I'm reading is true." I recommend praying like this because the Bible says, "If you seek Him, He will let you find Him" (1 Chronicles 28:9; Jeremiah 29:13; Psalm 145:18–19).

Thirdly, supplement your reading of the Gospels with these

two fantastic books: *The Case for Christ* and *The Case for Faith*, both by Lee Strobel, an award-winning journalist and former atheist. In these books, he interviews several historical experts who discuss the historical, archaeological, and scientific evidence for God's existence and Jesus's life. They also answer many of the common questions and objections that skeptics and atheists have. I think you'll find them both very helpful.

Fourthly, come to church with me on Sunday!

"Whatever you currently believe about Jesus of Nazareth, you owe it to yourself to investigate Him thoroughly. It makes little sense to ignore the one solitary life that continues to impact you in eternity if His claims are true."
–Frank Turek

11. "A loving God would never send people to Hell."

Mind if I ask you a question? What would people think of the local judge if he let unrepentant murderers, thieves, rapists, and child molesters go free and even rewarded them? Would people think the judge was loving? No. Throngs of people would protest at the courthouse, passionately yelling how *wrong* and *immoral* the judge was. They would be outraged over the lack of justice. And wouldn't you agree with them? It would be *unloving* of the judge to set criminals free and reward them. A good judge upholds the law. He locks up dangerous criminals. He quarantines them out of love for humanity and the wellbeing of his neighbors.

Well, like the good earthly judge, the Bible assures us that God, the loving, just Judge of the universe, is also going to judge people for their sins. The unrepentant, who turn away God's offer of forgiveness, will be quarantined in Hell, not only as just recompense for their crimes, but also to prevent them from ever again inflicting harm on others (Romans 2:5–6; Revelation 20:11–15).

But friend, realize this, a person won't end up in Hell because *God* sends him there. The person will have made the journey there himself. By that, I mean that Hell is the end of a long path (Matthew 7:13–14) that is chosen in this life, every day, as a person exercises his will.

Those who end up in Hell will have ignored the evidence for God that was made clear in creation (Romans 1:18–20). They will have resisted the convicting work of their consciences (Romans 2:14–15). They will have resisted the work of the Holy Spirit who convicts the world of sin (John 16:8). In many cases, they will have rejected God's messengers who shared God's offer of forgiveness with them (Matthew 23:34; Luke 11:49; Romans 8:36; Hebrews 11:37). They will have made it clear that they didn't want to know God. And they didn't want Jesus to be their Savior.

At the end of their lives, God will grant them the desire of their hearts, existence without God. But no God means no Heaven and none of the blessings He has for those who are with Him.

"There are only two kinds of people in the end: those who say to God, 'Thy will be done,' and those to whom God

says, in the end, 'Thy will be done.'"
–C. S. Lewis

"If you were to force people to do something against
their free choice, you would be dehumanizing them. The
option of forcing everyone to go to heaven is immoral, because
it's dehumanizing; it strips them of the dignity of making their
own decision; it denies them their freedom of choice; and it
treats them as a means to an end. When God allows people to
say 'no' to him, he actually respects and dignifies them."
–J. P. Moreland

12. "You Christians say the universe needs a maker because things don't just pop into existence from nothing. If that is the case, then God needs a maker! Who made God?"

Nobody made the God of the Bible. Unlike the finite physical universe that requires a creator, God does not need a creator. Why? Because God is eternal; He has always existed (Psalm 90:2). And He is immaterial, by that I mean He's a Spirit (John 4:24). He's not made up of physical parts that need assembly.

Now, before you scoff at the fact God has always existed, think through this with me. Something or someone *must* have always existed. Why? Well, follow the logic: If there ever was a time that absolutely nothing existed, nothing would exist now. But something *does* exist now. Therefore, there was never a time that absolutely nothing existed. So, I have no problem believing that *God* is the One who always existed. The universe, though, has not always existed;[23] and, therefore, requires a maker. Stars and planets don't just spring into existence from nothing.

13. "How can the Bible be true when it says the universe is only 6000 years old?"

Students of the Bible hold to a variety of opinions regarding the age of the universe. And the reason why is because the Bible doesn't specifically say the universe is 6000 years old. Even "young-Earth creationists" think the universe and the Earth could be closer to 10,000 years old. But a lot of Christian and Jewish scholars believe the first chapter of Genesis allows for a universe and Earth that is millions of years old. And all sides claim to have some scientific evidence on their side. So, we can't be sure about the exact age. But friend, don't let the ongoing debate over the age of the universe keep you from getting to know Jesus. There's not going to be a test on the Day of Judgment regarding how old the universe is. So, don't get hung up on that. What's important is that you have a relationship with your Creator. He made you, He loves you, and He wants to spend eternity with you. Call out to Him in prayer, confess your sin to Him, and get right with Him today by placing your faith in Jesus Christ.

....
23. The background radiation echo, the motion of the galaxies, and the second law of thermodynamics all point to the fact that the universe began to exist.

*"There are more sure marks of authenticity in the
Bible than in any profane [secular] history."*
–Isaac Newton

14. "The Biblical authors made several errors when they spoke about the natural world—I'll trust in science any day over your antiquated Bronze-Age collection of fables."

Thousands of archaeological discoveries and other historical evidences have shown that the Bible is certainly not a collection of fables.[24] But I find it interesting that you think the authors of the Bible made errors. Tell me about some of them.

There are books by scholars who discuss every alleged error in the Bible from beginning to end and explain where and how the critics have erred, not the Bible.[25] Would you be willing to read one?

Friend, about forty percent of professional natural scientists today are practicing Christians.[26] These scientists would say you have either misinterpreted the Bible or have put too much confidence in unsubstantiated theories. They have found the

....

24. See my articles, video, and book *Archaeological Evidence for the Bible* to learn about some of these evidences. Available here: alwaysbeready.com/archaeological-evidence-for-the-bible.

25. Go to alwaysbeready.com/bible-difficulties to access a plethora of free articles, videos, and books that address these alleged errors.

26. Jeffrey Burton Russell, *Exposing Myths About Christianity: A Guide to Answering 145 Viral Lies and Legends* (2012), 147. Jeffrey Burton Russell is Professor of History, Emeritus, at the University of California, Santa Barbara.

Bible to be in perfect harmony with testable, verifiable facts.

When one considers that the Bible was written long before the invention of satellites, telescopes, microscopes, deep-diving submarines, and so on, its accuracy is astounding! And not only were the authors accurate, they revealed several details about the Earth and the universe thousands of years before scientists discovered them.

For example, the first book of the Bible revealed that there are springs at the bottom of the ocean (Genesis 7:11; also Job 38:16). When deep-diving submarines were finally invented in the twentieth century, we discovered that revelation to be true.

About 4000 years ago, long before the ancient Greeks discovered the Earth was round, the Bible indicated that the Earth was a round sphere in Job 26:10.

The Bible also said that the Earth is completely unattached in open space in Job 26:7. We know that to be true now. But how would a Biblical author know that 4000 years ago? We believe God superintended the writing of the Bible to make sure its content accurately reflected the way things really are (2 Peter 1:21; 2 Timothy 3:16). Would you be interested in watching a video or reading a book wherein these details are discussed?[27] It very well may change your view of the Bible.

> *"He who reads the Bible to find fault with it will soon*
> *discover that the Bible finds fault with him."*
> **–Charles Spurgeon**

----

27. I recommend starting with my video, *The Bible's Scientific Accuracy and Foresight* (2018), and Lee Strobel's book, *The Case for a Creator* (2004).

15. "The universe is so vast! It's foolish to think a god built a universe billions of light years across just to have a personal relationship with you."

If you were God maybe you would have created a tiny little planet with no stars or galaxies for people to look up at and be amazed with. But God decided to create a massive universe full of billions of stars and interesting things for us to gaze at and explore. And I love that He did! If He had made a tiny universe with no other planets or stars, atheists would complain and say, "If God was really such a great and powerful creator, He should have made a massive universe and displayed His creative abilities!" But that is the very thing He *did* create! And atheists scoff. No matter what He did or does, those who want nothing to do with Him find fault. The rest of us will worship Him.

"I can see how it might be possible for a man to look down upon earth and be an atheist, but I cannot conceive how he could look up into the heavens and say that there is no God." **–Abraham Lincoln**

"The heavens proclaim the glory of God. The skies display his craftsmanship. Day after day they continue to speak; night after night they make him known. They speak without a sound or word; their voice is never heard. Yet their message has gone throughout the earth, and their words to all the world."
–**David** (Psalm 19:1–4)

16. "If God exists, why won't He just heal an amputee by restoring his limb? Then we would all know He exists!"[28]

Do you mean, perhaps, like the time Jesus miraculously restored the missing ear of a man in the Garden of Gethsemane (Luke 22:50–51)? Did the people repent and believe in Jesus when they beheld that miracle? No. They continued arresting Him, then led Him off to be brutally beaten and put to death on a cross the next morning.

Or how about the times Jesus raised dead people back to life (Luke 7:11–15, 8:41–55; John 11:1–44)? Those were greater miracles than restoring missing limbs. Surely, everyone would repent and believe in Jesus after those astounding miracles. No. Those who hated Jesus concluded that His miracles were accomplished by demonic powers (Matthew 12:24–28).

But what if Jesus empowered His followers to work miracles? Maybe people would believe in Him then? Well, that's the very thing Jesus did with His first disciples; He sent them

----
28. Some atheists on the Internet decided that a restored limb would be sufficient proof for God.

out to the world with the power to perform miracles (Matthew 10:8; Luke 10:1–19; Acts 3:1–11, 5:12–16). And they were subsequently put to death by people who didn't want to repent.

People who want to continue in sin are always able to find an excuse to reject God. So, miracles really aren't that effective at changing people's minds or hearts. They rarely produce the results atheists say they would (Luke 16:31).

Think about your own situation. Is your rejection of God really because of a lack of miracles? Or might you just desire to live without any accountability to a moral Lawgiver—God?

"Since atheists are unable to coherently support materialism, the heart of their case for atheism boils down to complaints about the way God does things: 'If I were God, I wouldn't do it this way. I wouldn't allow evil. I would have designed things differently. I would write everyone's name in the sky.'...But complaints are not arguments. A teenager may complain about a set of instructions his father left behind—the kid may want to do things completely differently. But that's not an argument for the non-existence or malice of the father."
–Frank Turek

"But he [Abraham] said to him [a certain rich man], 'If they do not listen to Moses and the Prophets, they will not be persuaded even if someone rises from the dead.'"
–Jesus (Luke 16:31)

17. "Evolution is a proven fact. I stopped believing in your imaginary sky daddy a long time ago!"

God is certainly not an "imaginary sky daddy," and you'll regret believing that when you stand before His throne on the Day of Judgment (Hebrews 10:31). But may I ask you a question? You seem like you're an open-minded individual. What are some of the books you've read wherein the author sought to lay out some of the major flaws with the theory of evolution? Oh, you haven't read any? Hmm, I thought you would have examined what hundreds of scientists believe are fatal flaws with the theory of evolution before settling down so confidently in favor of it.

What flaws? you ask. How about the fossil record? If evolution really is the explanation for all of life, the fossil record should show continuous and gradual changes from the bottom layer to the top layers. But it doesn't. Nearly all groups of animals appear suddenly, simultaneously, and fully developed in the fossil record. This alone is devastating to the theory.

But let me get this straight. You think it's absurd to believe there's a creative intelligence behind the universe. But you believe it's more reasonable to believe that once there was nothing and that nothingness turned itself into all the stars, planets, and eventually living organisms? Interesting.

Have you done an in-depth study on the complexities of the human body? I have a hard time believing male and female humans came into existence without any kind of designer involved. Think this through with me. The human body has 206 bones,[29] about 700 muscles,[30] hearts that beat over 100,000 times a day,[31] and eyes made up of two million parts.[32] I can't even fathom the kind of faith it would take to believe all those parts found each other and assembled themselves.

What do you think evolved first, the human heart with all its valves and chambers, or the blood, or the veins? They all work together and are dependent on each other to keep the body alive. They certainly couldn't have all come together at the same time, apart from a creator. So, what evolved first, and how did the first creature that managed to grow a heart chamber or a vein survive for thousands of years before the other stuff managed to evolve?

And what about the trillions of cells that make up your body? Bill Gates said that the DNA in the cells is like a computer program but far more advanced than any software Microsoft has ever created.[33] How did that information get into the cells? Computer programs never write themselves. There is always a programmer involved.

Oh, the ape-men fossils are proof of evolution? Surely, they aren't! "Piltdown man" turned out to be a colossal hoax. With

....
29. Donald Rizzo, *Fundamentals of Anatomy and Physiology* (2016), 175.

30. Innerbody, "Muscular System," http://www.innerbody.com/image/musfov.html.

31. Arkansas Heart Hospital, "Amazing Heart Facts," https://www.arheart.com/heart-health/amazing-heart-facts.

32. "The Eye is One of the Most Complex Organisms in the Human Body," https://www.eyeinstitute.co.nz/About-eyes.

33. Bill Gates, *The Road Ahead* (1996), 228.

the help of DNA technology, we've learned that "Neanderthals" were humans, not ape-men or ancestors of modern humans. "Nebraska man" turned out to be a pig. "Lucy," apparently, was a chimpanzee. "Ida," once hailed as the "missing link in human evolution" was more recently reclassified as a small, tailed, extinct primate and ancestor of Lemurs, not humans![34] Friend, the theory of evolution is a materialistic creation-myth masquerading as science. Would you be willing to read a good book or two on this topic?[35]

"The extreme rarity of transitional forms in the fossil record persists as the trade secret of paleontology. The evolutionary trees that adorn our textbooks have data only at the tips and nodes of their branches; the rest is inference, however reasonable, not the evidence of fossils."
–Stephen Jay Gould

"Natural selection may be able to explain the survival of a species, but it cannot explain the arrival of a species."
–Norman Geisler

"The positive evidence for Darwinism is confined to small-scale evolutionary changes like insects developing insecticide resistance....Evidence like that for insecticide resistance confirms the Darwinian selection mechanism for small-scale changes,

....

34. Marvin Lubenow discusses these and other so-called "ape-men" in his excellent book *Bones of Contention: A Creationist Assessment of Human Fossils* (2004).

35. Two excellent books: Jonathan Wells, *Icons of Evolution: Why Much of What We Teach About Evolution is Wrong* (2000); Lee Strobel, *The Case for a Creator* (2004).

but hardly warrants the grand extrapolation that Darwinists want. It is a huge leap going from insects developing insecticide resistance via the Darwinian mechanism of natural selection and random variation to the very emergence of insects in the first place by that same mechanism."
–William Dembski

"The tragedy is that evolution is a nineteenth-century philosophy that has been destroyed by twentieth-century science. Yet the lie continues to be perpetrated, not on scientific grounds, but because it is what morally justifies our immoral society today."
–Ron Carlson

18. "Religions, Christianity included, are responsible for most of the world's wars, suffering, and atrocities!"

Unfortunately, misguided religious people have caused a lot of suffering, but so have atheists and non-religious people. Joseph Stalin, Adolf Hitler, and Mao Zedong murdered as many as 100 million people in just a few decades of the twentieth century—far more than those who were put to death by theists of any stripe over the past 500 years![36]

Friend, if people would follow the teachings of Jesus, the

....
36. Frank Turek, *Stealing From God: Why Atheists Need God to Make Their Case* (2014), 119; Greg Koukl, "The Real Murderers: Atheism or Christianity?" https://www.str.org/articles/the-real-murderers-atheism-or-christianity.

world would be much more loving. He taught us to love and treat others like *we* want to be loved and treated (Matthew 5:44, 7:12). So, it would be a mistake to blame Jesus for the world's wars, suffering, and atrocities. But may I ask you a question?

Haven't you, by some of your own actions, caused some of the world's suffering? Have you ever hurt someone's feelings, been rude, short-tempered, or acted selfishly? Yes? Well, then *you're* part of the problem. And so am I. We've all sinned and brought hurt upon others (Romans 3:10, 23). Thankfully though, God has a plan in place for an incredible "new earth" where there will be no more suffering, no more death, no more wars (2 Peter 3:13; Revelation 21:1-4). Would you like to live in a world like that? You can. God has a glorious future in store for all those who have been redeemed and forgiven of their sins.

Do you want God to forgive you for your sins? He can do that because Jesus, God Himself, died on a cruel wooden cross to take the punishment for your sins. Three days later He rose from the grave. If you'll look to Him, if you'll put your trust in Him and what He did for you, you'll be forgiven and granted "everlasting life" (John 3:16). That's the incredible news of the gospel.

"Critiquing bad religion is not something that Christopher Hitchens first dreamt up as he sat down at his word processor one evening to bang out God Is Not Great. *That religions sometimes can go badly wrong is a much older point, indeed one made some 2,000 years earlier by Jesus himself. His most frequent clashes were with the religious leaders of his day,*

42

whom he accused of using religion for personal gain, or as a tool to exploit and to marginalize. In short, if you're going to criticize religion when it goes wrong, you're probably closer to Jesus on that issue than you might ever have imagined."
–Andy Bannister

"If there is a root of evil that became a terrifying force that almost brought the world to destruction in the first half of the twentieth century, it is the anti-religious ideologies of Germany and Russia, North Vietnam, and North Korea. It takes almost willful blindness to invert this historical fact, and to suppose that the religions that were persecuted and crushed by these brutal forces are the real sources of evil in the world...So the value judgment put forth by atheists that "atheism is good and Christianity is evil" is not only logically faulty because good and evil don't exist in an atheistic world—it's also empirically false!"
–Keith Ward and **Frank Turek**

19. "The Bible has been tampered with and changed so many times down through the centuries, we can't trust it today, even if it was once trustworthy."

It sounds like you've done some serious research on this. Just curious, what are some of the books you've read on the transmission of the Biblical text?

Well, fortunately, this popular claim isn't true. To show that the Bible has been tampered with and changed, critics would have to be able to point to ancient copies of the Bible and show us what they used to say, and then show us the differences in what the Bible says now. But that's the very thing critics can't do, because our modern copies of the Bible say what the ancient copies say. And for good reason! Our modern Bibles are translated directly from the ancient manuscript copies of the Bible.[37]

In addition to this, we can also compare our modern Bibles to the surviving writings of Christians in the second and third century. They quoted the text of the Bible thousands of times in their writings.[38] And when we compare our Bibles to their ancient quotations of the Bible, we see again that the Bibles we use today are accurate copies of the Bible the early church used.

20. "The world is a mess! To think there is a loving God who allows all the evil and suffering that takes place is preposterous!"

It's interesting to me that you interpret evil and suffering to mean there is no God. What do you chalk up all the good days, good health, family, friends, pleasurable experiences, and

---

37. For an excellent treatment of how the Bible was copied, preserved, and passed down to us, see Norman Geisler and William Nix, *From God to Us: How We Got Our Bible* (2012), Revised and Expanded Edition.

38. Ibid., 138, 217–218.

flavorful food to? It seems to me that there is a lot in the world that points *to* a benevolent Creator (Acts 14:16–17; Romans 1:19–21).

The world *does* have some problems, that's for sure, but life could certainly be a lot worse. A lot of the suffering we witness is the result of mankind's sin and rebellion against God. Imagine how much better life on the planet could be if there were no iron-fisted dictators, terrorists, criminals, corrupt politicians, gangs, drug dealers, drunk drivers, absent parents, child molesters, schoolyard bullies, etc. Think of the billions of dollars that could be spent improving the quality of life for people if that money didn't have to be spent fighting crime and other evils.

Friend, that kind of life is coming. The Bible says God will put a stop to evil (2 Peter 3:7–13). He is going to judge people for their sins, quarantine unrepentant evildoers, and create a new earth for His people where there will no longer be any death, mourning, crying, or pain (Revelation 21:1–4). In the meantime, God is working out much good amid the suffering (Genesis 50:20; Romans 8:28; Philippians 1:12). For example, suffering people often turn to God and receive the kind of help they truly need: a sin-cleansing, soul-saving relationship with God. And I urge you to turn to Him as well.

"The believer in God must explain one thing, the existence of sufferings; the nonbeliever, however, must explain the existence of everything else."
–Dennis Prager

21. "What about countries where hundreds of thousands of people are starving? What kind of God would create a planet that would put people through that kind of horrendous suffering? Certainly, not a loving one!"

Well, our hearts ache for those suffering in that way. And Christians are doing a lot of great work in the world to alleviate their suffering. But friend, the lack of food is not due to a faulty ecosystem that doesn't produce enough food to meet human need. As of 2014, the world was producing enough food to feed 10 billion people.[39] The lack of food in certain areas is often because of wars, or governments and rebel forces not permitting food, aid, and supplies to reach the people. It's not *God* who is cruel, but humans who disobey God's instructions to love our neighbors and look out for the interest of others (Mark 12:31; Philippians 2:4).

You seem upset with God about the food shortage. Do you ever thank God for the daily meals He provides you? You claim God must be cruel (if He exists) for allowing people to go hungry. Do you help at your local soup kitchen or in some other way to feed the hungry in your city? Does that mean you're cruel?

---

39. Eric Holt Gimenez, "We Already Grow Enough Food For 10 Billion People—and Still Can't End Hunger," *Huffington Post*, https://www.huffingtonpost.com/eric-holt-gimenez/world-hunger_b_1463429.html, December 18, 2014.

"Let us remember that every worldview—not just Christianity's—must give an explanation or an answer for evil and suffering...this is not just a problem distinctive to Christianity. It will not do for the challenger just to raise the question. This problem of evil is one to which we all must offer an answer, regardless of the belief system to which we subscribe." –**Ravi Zacharias**

22. "Only a cruel God would stand by and allow young innocent babies to die!"

You mean the millions of babies that humans put to death every year in abortion clinics? Oh, other babies. I'm sorry. I misunderstood you.

Can I ask you a couple of questions? Are you an atheist? It seems to me most atheists believe a woman has a right to get an abortion. Would this describe your position? Yes?

Okay, so, maybe you can help me understand this. Pro-choice adherents believe a woman has the right to bring a viable third-trimester baby in her womb to an abortion clinic, where a doctor will puncture the baby's skull with scissors or take a large needle and inject a lethal dose of digoxin or potassium chloride into the baby's beating heart to cause cardiac arrest. And then, depending on the type of abortion, the abortionist will tear apart the baby's body with forceps to make his or her removal easier, then throw the baby's body in the trash. That's morally justifiable to pro-choice adherents. But they also complain, "If God exists, He's a cruel god because

He stands by and allows innocent babies to die!" I'm curious how you justify that position—that humans have the *right* to put babies to death, but God is *cruel* for allowing babies to die.

> "Ronald Reagan once quipped, "I've noticed all those in favor of abortion are already born." Indeed, all pro-abortionists would become pro-life immediately if they found themselves back in the womb."
> –**Norman Geisler**

23. "There's no evidence Jesus ever existed!"

How did you come to that conclusion? Have you done any careful research on this? The reason I ask is because there is a wealth of evidence Jesus was a real person. So much evidence, historians consider His existence beyond dispute.[40]

Consider this. In addition to the 27 New Testament documents that tell us about Jesus's life, more than 30 historical sources *outside* of the Bible mention Him within a century and a half of His life. I'm talking about sources like the first century historian Flavius Josephus, Roman historians like Cornelius Tacitus and Suetonius, and a collection of Jewish writings called the Talmud.

....
40. Even Bart Ehrman, the well-known critic of the Bible, acknowledges, "With respect to Jesus, we have numerous, independent accounts of his life...sources that originated in Jesus' native tongue...and that can be dated to within just a year or two of his life...Historical sources like that are pretty astounding for an ancient figure of any kind...The claim that Jesus was simply made up falters on every ground." https://www.huffingtonpost.com/bart-d-ehrman/did-jesus-exist_b_1349544.html.

These ancient sources don't just *mention* Jesus, they *confirm* more than a hundred details recorded about Jesus in the New Testament.[41] For example, Josephus confirms that Jesus was "a doer of amazing deeds," that Pontius "Pilate condemned Him to be crucified to die," that He was a teacher who "won over many Jews and many of the Greeks," and that Jesus's disciples "reported that he had appeared to them three days after his crucifixion and that he was alive."[42] The Talmud confirms that Jesus was put to death at the time of the Passover Feast, just like the Bible says.[43]

The evidence for Jesus is there for those willing to look at it. I encourage you to read the New Testament accounts of His life and get to know Him.

"If one believes in the existence of Socrates, Alexander the Great, or Julius Caesar, then one should definitely believe in Christ's existence. If historicity is established by written records in multiple copies that date originally from near contemporaneous sources, there is far more historical evidence for Christ's existence than for any of theirs. The historicity of Christ is attested not only by Christians but also by Greek, Roman, and Jewish Sources."
–Josh McDowell and Dave Sterrett

....

41. Gary Habermas documents these sources and comments on the details in his book *The Historical Jesus: Ancient Evidence for the Life of Christ*. Also see Norman Geisler, *Baker Encyclopedia of Apologetics* (1999), 381–385; F. F. Bruce, *Jesus and Christian Origins Outside the New Testament*.

42. Josephus, *Antiquities of the Jews*, Book 18, Chapter 3:3.

43. Babylonian Talmud, Sanhedrin 43a.

24. "The New Testament authors stole the whole idea for Jesus's virgin birth from ancient religions like Mithraism."

Friend, have you studied ancient religions? Tell me a little bit about the ancient Persian religion of Mithraism. What was the name of its mythological deity? I'm open to learning. Oh, you really haven't studied it?

Mithras, the name of Mithraism's deity, was not thought of as having been born of a virgin in any of the most ancient myths. The myths say Mithras arose spontaneously from a rock in a cave.[44] Does that sound like a virgin birth to you? No.

Jesus's birth to a virgin, as recorded in the New Testament (Matthew 1:18; Luke 1:34), was not hijacked from Mithraism. It was the fulfillment of Old Testament prophecies in the Books of Genesis (3:15) and Isaiah (7:14), both penned centuries before Jesus was born.

Have you studied Biblical prophecies? Fulfilled prophecies are an incredible evidence that the Biblical authors spoke with the supernatural aid of someone who knew future events with absolute certainty (Isaiah 46:9–10). For example, centuries before Jesus was born, Jewish prophets revealed that Bethlehem would be where Jesus would be born (Micah 5:2). They foretold the family line He'd be born into (Genesis 12:1–3, 2 Samuel 7:12f), the kinds of miracles He would perform

....
44. Ronald Nash, *The Gospel and the Greeks: Did the New Testament Borrow from Pagan Thought?* (2003), 134; Edwin Yamauchi, *Persia and the Bible* (1990), 498; Lee Strobel, *The Case for the Real Jesus* (2007), 170–171.

(Isaiah 35:5–6), how and why He would be rejected and put to death (Psalm 22:16–18; Isaiah 53:3f), the year He would be put to death (Daniel 9:24–26), and that He'd rise from the grave (Psalm 16:10; Isaiah 53:10). Jesus fulfilled all those predictions, and many more, to the tee.[45]

If I give you a Bible with some of these prophecies highlighted, would you be willing to look at them?

"For we did not follow cleverly devised myths when we made known to you the power and coming of our Lord Jesus Christ, but we were eyewitnesses of his majesty."
–Peter (2 Peter 1:16)

"Always remember that Jesus commanded his followers to go into the world and make disciples, not simply win arguments."
–Andy Bannister

25. "Jesus's disciples made up the stories about His miracles."

Friend, help me understand your worldview. Do you believe in God? No? So, in your godless universe, miracles aren't even possible. So, it seems to me that someone with your worldview might reject Jesus's miracles before even considering the evidence. Is that the case with you? Have you rejected Jesus's miracles before thinking through the evidence for them? What

45. See "Chart of Old Testament Prophecies Fulfilled in the Life of Christ" at alwaysbeready.com/evidence-for-jesus; and John Walvoord, *Every Prophecy About Jesus*.

books have you read wherein the evidence is discussed?

If Jesus's disciples invented the accounts of His miracles, what do you think their motivation was? What were some of the benefits or advantages they received for lying? Liars lie to get out of trouble or gain some type of advantage or benefit. But what the early Christians said about Jesus, didn't get them *out* of trouble or result in any kind of benefit. The things they said and wrote about Jesus got them *in* trouble. What they received from the Jewish and Roman authorities was rejection, persecution, imprisonment, torture, and martyrdom.[46] Do you think they'd make up lies to bring all that suffering upon themselves? I have a hard time believing that.

"All I am in private life is a literary critic and historian, that's my job...And I'm prepared to say on that basis if anyone thinks the Gospels are either legends or novels, then that person is simply showing his incompetence as a literary critic. I've read a great many novels and I know a fair amount about the legends that grew up among early people, and I know perfectly well the Gospels are not that kind of stuff."
–C. S. Lewis

....
46. Luke discusses this in the Book of Acts (4:18, 7:58, 12:2–5, 14:19, 16:22–24, 17:5–8, 24:27). This sort of treatment of early Christians is also confirmed *outside* the New Testament in the writings of Flavius Josephus, Eusebius, Tertullian, Hegesippus, Polycarp, Ignatius, Cornelius Tacitus, Dionysius, Clement of Alexandria, Clement of Rome, and Origen. For a good overview of these sources and what they said regarding this matter, see Gary Habermas and Michael Licona, *The Case for the Resurrection of Jesus* (2004), 56–62.

26. "There's no evidence Jesus rose from the grave!"

I'm curious. Have you looked at the evidence Christians say exists, or have you just assumed there's no evidence? What arguments or evidence did you find unconvincing? Why?

I think there's good evidence for Jesus's resurrection. Imagine with me for a moment that the year is 1963. You happen to be in the city of Dallas for work. You hear that President John F. Kennedy is going to be driving through the city in a motorcade on his way to give a speech. So, you go. As the President nears where you and hundreds of others are standing, the infamous shots ring out, and sadly, you witness the assassination of our 35th President.

Question for you. How hard would it have been in the weeks following that tragic event, to convince thousands of people in the city of Dallas who witnessed the assassination, that J.F.K. came back to life and walked out of his grave? Pretty much impossible, right? You might convince a couple people, but you'd have an incredibly hard time convincing thousands of people. Why? People don't rise from the grave.

Well, the same was true in Israel in the first century. People didn't just walk out of their graves.[47] And yet, in the days immediately following Jesus's crucifixion,[48] thousands of Jews who lived in Jerusalem and who knew Jesus had died,

47. Except for Lazarus (John 11:43–44) who was raised by Jesus, and "the saints" (Matthew 27:50–53) God raised at the time of Jesus's resurrection.

48. Jesus's crucifixion is mentioned by Roman and Jewish historians *outside* the New Testament, e.g., Flavius Josephus, Cornelius Tacitus, Jewish Talmud.

suddenly converted to Christianity, convinced Jesus rose from the grave.[49] How does one explain that apart from Jesus's resurrection? Do you really think thousands of people in those early days were deceived into thinking a man rose from the dead?

Maybe Jesus's disciples stole Jesus's body from the tomb? Why would they do that? And if they had a dead corpse on their hands, how were they able to convince thousands of people He rose from the grave? Maybe prop him up at a table for a press conference, but answer all the questions for Him? Friend, the "stolen body theory" doesn't work as an adequate explanation for the empty tomb.

If I were to give you a book that explains the evidence for Jesus's life, death, and resurrection, would you be willing to read it?[50]

"What did the Jewish New Testament writers have to gain by making up a new religion? By insisting the Resurrection occurred, they got excommunicated from the synagogue and then beaten, tortured, and killed. Last I checked that was not a list of perks."

–Frank Turek

---

49. Luke, whose writings have been confirmed by numerous historical investigations and archaeological discoveries, tells us that 3000 people believed the first post-resurrection sermon preached a few minutes' walk from Jesus's tomb (Acts 2:41). In Acts 4:4, Luke said there were 5000 believers comprising the early Christian church in Jerusalem. In Acts 6:7, Luke says the number of disciples "continued to increase greatly in Jerusalem."

50. Lee Strobel, *The Case for Christ: A Journalist's Personal Investigation of the Evidence for Jesus* (2016), *Updated and Expanded Edition.*

"I know the resurrection is a fact, and Watergate proved it to me. How? Because 12 men testified they had seen Jesus raised from the dead, then they proclaimed that truth for 40 years, never once denying it. Every one was beaten, tortured, stoned and put in prison. They would not have endured that if it weren't true. Watergate embroiled 12 of the most powerful men in the world—and they couldn't keep a lie for three weeks. You're telling me 12 apostles could keep a lie for 40 years? Absolutely impossible."

–Charles Colson

"The disciples had nothing to gain by lying and starting a new religion. They faced hardship, ridicule, hostility, and martyr's deaths. In light of this, they could never have sustained such unwavering motivation if they knew what they were preaching was a lie. The disciples were not fools and Paul was a cool-headed intellectual of the first rank. There would have been several opportunities over three to four decades of ministry to reconsider and renounce a lie."

–J. P. Moreland

27. "It's outrageous to think God would only save people who have a relationship with Jesus!"

I think it's outrageous that God would save any of us. Friend, none of us deserve salvation. We deserve judgment and death. After all the sinful things we've done, it's incredibly merciful and gracious of God to make a way of salvation possible at all.

Let's imagine some stranger comes over to you right now and unprovoked by anything you've done, spits in your face, screams vulgarities at you, and kicks you. Then he walks away. He doesn't apologize. He doesn't ask for forgiveness.

Later this week, you're planning a big feast, barbecuing for friends and family. Would you invite that guy? No. And you certainly wouldn't force him to come against his will. Why not? There hasn't been any reconciliation or forgiveness. There hasn't been any repentance. And that guy doesn't even like you. In fact, he hates you.

Well, this is why some people won't be at *God's* feast ("the marriage supper of the Lamb" Revelation 19:9) in His kingdom. They're like the guy who came up and kicked you. But they've kicked God! By that I mean they've spurned His instructions, trampled on His Word, sinned against Him, and walked away. They haven't apologized. They've laughed at His offer of forgiveness. And they want nothing to do with Him.

God, who is more loving than us, still sends them an invitation (Matthew 22:1–14) and says 'Come, you're invited to a great feast I'm throwing. I love you! I will forgive you.' But they mock and persecute His messengers, and tear up the invitations. They don't want to be reconciled to God. They don't love Him, and they don't want to know Him. There are a hundred things they'd rather do on a Sunday than spend an hour at church.

Friend, God is *not* going to force people like that to spend eternity with Him.

"A man who was merely a man and said the sort of things Jesus said would not be a great moral teacher. He would either be a lunatic—on the level with the man who says he is a poached egg—or else he would be the Devil of Hell. You must make your choice. Either this man was, and is, the Son of God: or else a madman or something worse. You can shut Him up for a fool, you can spit at Him and kill Him as a demon; or you can fall at His feet and call Him Lord and God. But let us not come with any patronizing nonsense about His being a great human teacher. He has not left that open to us. He did not intend to."

–C. S. Lewis

28. "Jesus's earliest followers never thought of Him as God!"

I'm curious why you would say that. Have you read the Gospels? If I was to show you actual quotes by Jesus's earliest followers referring to Him as God, would you be willing to change your mind?

For example, Peter called Jesus "Our God and Savior" in 2 Peter 1:1. John called Jesus "God" in John 1:1. Thomas called Jesus "My Lord and my God!" in John 20:28. Paul called Jesus "Our great God and Savior" in Titus 2:13. And these kinds of references to Jesus's deity in the first century didn't stop with the original disciples. The leaders of the Christian church in the second and third centuries continued to affirm this very same teaching. Well-respected leaders like Ignatius, Justin Martyr, Polycarp, and Irenaeus refer to Jesus as God over and over in their writings.[51]

> *"If you are drawn into controversy, use very hard arguments and very soft words. Frequently you cannot convince a man by tugging at his reason, but you can persuade him by winning his affections."*
> **–Charles Spurgeon**

29. "The Gospels are full of contradictions!"

Oh, I disagree. I have a Bible here on my phone. Let's look at a couple. What examples would you like to discuss?

Friend, there may be a handful of verses in the Gospels that appear to you to be at odds with one another. But with a little investigation into the contexts of the passages or the cultural and geographical settings, they are easily explained. For example, critics say there's a contradiction in the Gospels concerning where Jesus healed a blind man.

Luke 18:35 says Jesus healed him "as He was approaching Jericho." But Mark 10:46 says He healed the man "as He went out of Jericho." So, critics say, "Surely Luke or Mark made a mistake. They can't both be right." And that appears to be the case, until you do a little homework and find out that an archaeologist named Ernst Sellin discovered "The Twin-Cities of Jericho" in Jesus's time. There was the old city of Jericho

---

51. Nathan Busenitz, Professor of Historical Theology at The Master's Seminary, provides a great sampling of their quotes in his article: "Did the Early Church Affirm Jesus' Deity?" http://thecripplegate.com/did-the-early-church-affirm-jesus-deity.

(destroyed in the Book of Joshua, but rebuilt in 1 Kings 16:34) and there was the new Roman city of Jericho. There were two cities called "Jericho," separated from one another by about a mile.[52] Knowing this solves the dilemma. It's likely that Luke referred to one of the cities and Mark referred to the other. A plausible explanation is that the miracle took place *between* the two cities (Mark mentioning the city Jesus had just left, Luke mentioning the city Jesus was approaching).

Would you be willing to read an article or book that explains more of these alleged contradictions in the Bible?[53] There are good explanations for every one of them.

> *"Men do not reject the Bible because it contradicts itself, but because it contradicts them."*
> **–E. Paul Hovey**

30. "The Gospels were written down 300 years after Jesus lived!"

I'm interested to hear how you came to that conclusion. Have you studied early church history? What are some of the good books you've read on the topic?

Friend, there's no evidence any of the New Testament books

....

52. Joseph Free, *Archaeology and Bible History, Revised Edition* (1992), 251; John McRay, *Archaeology and the New Testament* (1991), 17; Bryant G. Wood, "The Walls of Jericho," http://www.biblearchaeology.org/post/2008/06/The-Walls-of-Jericho. aspx#Article.

53. See my article, "Are There Contradictions in the Gospels?" at alwaysbeready. com/bible-difficulties. For a more in-depth treatment, I suggest *The Big Book of Bible Difficulties* by Norman Geisler and Thomas Howe, and *The Bible Handbook of Difficult Verses* by Josh McDowell and Sean McDowell.

were written down three hundred years after Jesus. And there's good evidence most of the New Testament was completed before AD 70—within 40 years of Jesus's life.

Take, for example, the destruction of the Jewish temple in Jerusalem by the Romans in AD 70. Their temple took decades to build (John 2:20). It was the center of religious activity for the Jews. But after the Jews revolted against Roman rule, Roman soldiers besieged the city of Jerusalem, broke through the walls, slaughtered thousands of Jews and destroyed the temple.[54] This was one of the most momentous events in all Jewish history. One would expect to find some mention of it in the New Testament if it had been written after the year AD 70. But there's not a word.

Another evidence most of the New Testament was completed within a short time of Jesus's life is its silence about Peter and Paul's deaths. We know from historical sources outside the Bible that Paul was put to death around AD 64 and Peter around AD 65.[55] If the New Testament was penned after their deaths, we would expect to at least find a brief mention of their passing in the New Testament. Why? Peter and Paul were two of Jesus's most influential followers. And the New Testament tells us about the deaths of other early Christians, for example, Stephen's stoning (Acts 7:59–60) and James's murder by a sword (Acts 12:2).

Friend, you can be confident that the New Testament was

....
54. Christian History Institute, "70 Titus Destroys Jerusalem," https://christianhistoryinstitute.org/magazine/article/titus-destroys-jerusalem.

55. Eusebius, *Ecclesiastical History*, Book 2, Chapter 25:1–8; B. K. Kuiper, *The Church in History* (1964), 8.

written down in the first century and is a trustworthy account of Jesus's life.

"The fact that the first three Gospels were written prior to the fall of Jerusalem in AD 70 and the Gospel of John not long thereafter, makes impossible the attempt of liberal Bible critics and secularists to argue that they are the product of a developing oral tradition in which the early church modified Jesus' life and teachings."
–John Montgomery

31. "The New Testament doesn't tell us the whole truth about Jesus. Christians purposely left other writings about Him out of the New Testament, for example, *The Gospel of Judas* and *The Gospel of Thomas*."

Tell me what you know about the so-called *Gospel of Thomas* or *Judas*. Do you know *who* wrote either of them? Do you know *when* they were written? Why do you think Christians left those books out of the New Testament?

Scholars have determined that both of those writings were written in the second or third century, long after Thomas and Judas died.[56] So, they weren't written by eyewitnesses of Jesus's

----

56. See Lee Strobel's interview with Craig Evans in *The Case for the Real Jesus* (2007), 23–63; Norman Geisler, "Gospel of Thomas" and "Nag Hammadi Gospels," *The Big Book of Christian Apologetics* (2012), 211–212, 380–381; Darrell Bock, *The*

life, nor the disciples they're named after. That's one strike against their reliability.

A second strike against them is their content. The writings contain bizarre sayings and details that flatly contradict the earlier authentic teachings of Jesus, as recorded in the New Testament.

For example, in *The Gospel of Thomas*, Peter says females don't deserve life.[57] And Jesus talks about the importance of women making themselves into males so that they can go to Heaven![58] How bizarre is that? *The Gospel of Judas* portrays Judas, the one who betrayed Jesus in the New Testament, as a hero who will one day rule over humanity.[59]

So, Christians recognized these writings for what they were, spurious and untrustworthy. Wanting to preserve the truth about Jesus, they purposely left these writings out of the Bible. And I'm thankful they did!

Friend, if you want to know who Jesus really was, we have accurate accounts of His life and teachings in the New Testament. Would you be willing to read the Gospels if I gave you a Bible?

Missing Gospels: Unearthing the Truth Behind Alternative Christianities.

57. *The Gospel of Thomas*, 114, http://gnosis.org/naghamm/gthlamb.html.

58. Ibid.

59. *The Gospel of Judas*, 46, 56, http://www.nytimes.com/packages/pdf/national/judastxt.pdf.

32. "It's ridiculous to think that all the races, with their different skin colors, came from Noah's family!"

It sounds like you've read some of the Bible. Mind if I ask you a couple questions? I gather that you are an atheist. Is that true? What do you think would be easier: A. For nothing to turn itself into something? Or B. For something that already exists to slowly make some tiny adaptations in response to different environmental pressures? If you say B, then you should find it easier to accept the Biblical account than the popular atheistic alternative. Why? The atheistic view proposed by Stephen Hawking, Richard Dawkins, and others is that billions of multi-colored galaxies (and people millions of years later), sprang into existence from "nothing."[60] Friend, that is irrational. Nothing does not produce something.

I find the Biblical account of Noah's descendants developing different shades of skin as they spread out and settled in different parts of the ancient world much easier to believe. It's likely that the groups that settled in colder climates (such as northern Europe), where there is not much sunlight, developed fairer skin. The people groups who settled nearer to the equator (like in Africa), where the sunlight is more intense, developed darker skin.

The different people groups that exist today are not different "races." There is only one race—the human race (Acts

---
60. Stephen Hawking, *The Grand Design* (2012), 180; Richard Dawkins, "Something from Nothing and the Magic of Reality–Part 2," http://www.youtube.com/watch?v=ygXDWOp2vgs.

17:26). The differences between Chinese people, Eskimos, Indians, Caucasians, Australian Aborigines, and so on, are only skin deep. We are all humans with 206 bones,[61] about 700 muscles,[62] and the exact same organs. The only significant difference between us is the shade of our skin (some have more melanin in their skin than others).

33. "There are so many different translations of the Bible, no one could possibly know which one to trust!"

Have you read some of the different translations? What were some of the differences you spotted? Were there any doctrinal differences between the translations? No? Friend, just about any English translation of the Bible you read today is going to teach the same thing about Jesus, Heaven, Hell, the free gift of everlasting life, and so on.[63]

One of the reasons there are Bibles with slightly different wording is because they were translated into English by different publishers who had different goals. Some had the goal of publishing a more readable, easier-to-understand edition. Other publishers had the goal of translating the Hebrew and Greek language as literally as possible.

....

61. Donald Rizzo, *Fundamentals of Anatomy and Physiology* (2016), 175.

62. Innerbody, "Muscular System," http://www.innerbody.com/image/musfov.html.

63. I have in mind here the ESV, NASB, NET, KJV, NKJV, NIV, and NLT. *The New World Translation* published by the Jehovah's Witnesses cult is a fraudulent translation that is not faithful to the original languages in several places.

Another reason there are different translations is because there are often several English words that a Greek or Hebrew word can be translated into. And so, some translations might use the word *difficulty* or *hardship*, whereas another translation might say *trial*, *trouble*, or *tribulation*. But the same truth still comes through.

If I were to give you an easy-to-understand translation of the New Testament, would you be willing to read it?[64] If you'd like, we could get together for coffee and talk about what you're reading. I think you're going to find Jesus fascinating!

34. "You can't be sure of what the Bible means. Look at all the Christian denominations. Even they disagree about what to believe!"

Christians agree on far more than some realize. For example, we agree on the authenticity of the Bible, who Jesus was, what His death on the cross accomplished, that Jesus rose from the grave, that He's coming again to judge the world. There is great consensus amongst Christians on those major doctrinal matters.

Some Christians disagree on peripheral debatable matters (the age of the earth, or how church leadership should be structured). But don't let our disagreements on things that

---

64. *The New Living Translation* is a good one. Greg Laurie's ministry, Harvest, publishes a "New Believer's Bible," an inexpensive paperback that has fantastic notes in it to guide new believers: https://www.harvest.org/store/new-believers-bible-new-testament.

won't matter in eternity keep you from a relationship with God and having your sins forgiven.

Have you read the New Testament? What didn't you understand? Would you be willing to reread it? If you get stuck on a passage, you can email me or we can get together for lunch and I'll try my best to clarify what it says. But I think you'll be surprised with how much of it is easy to understand!

35. "Churches are full of hypocrites!"

There probably are some hypocrites in every church, but if the Bible is faithfully taught where they attend, what a great place for them to be! They'll learn that hypocrisy is wrong (Matthew 23:28; 1 Peter 2:1). And perhaps they will repent.

Mind if I ask you a couple questions? Are you an atheist? Do you really think hypocrisy is wrong? Why do you think it's wrong? In an atheistic universe where there is no moral lawgiver, no God, there *are* no real rights and wrongs, just opinions. So, I'm wondering why you think hypocrisy is actually wrong.

If it's truly wrong, there must be a moral lawgiver. Would you be willing to concede that? If there's a moral lawgiver, it's likely that you have broken some of His laws. Are you familiar with the Ten Commandments in the Bible? Have you obeyed them? Have you ever stolen anything? Lied? Slept with someone you weren't married to?

Friend, don't allow someone else's sin (like hypocrisy) keep you from receiving God's forgiveness for your own sins. God will deal with the hypocrites (Matthew 24:51). But one day, you too are going to stand before God to give an account for your sins (Romans 14:12). Bringing up hypocrites with God isn't going to do anything to remove your guilt. You need to place your faith in Jesus for that to happen.

"If you deny the existence of God, any moral values you advocate for are nothing more than your personal preferences."
–Andy Bannister

36. "Why do you Christians persist in judging people when Jesus said not to judge?"

Actually, Jesus didn't forbid judging. In John 7:24, He said, "Do not judge according to appearance, *but judge with righteous judgment.*" Friend, it's impossible to go through life without judging. You'd be dead if you weren't regularly making judgments about where to go, what to eat, who to befriend, what to keep a safe distance from. And God knows that. So, Jesus says, "Judge" but judge *righteously.* How do we do that?

Christians consult with what God has revealed in the Bible. And then we carefully try to align our view, our assessment of a person or activity, with what the Bible says. And seeing that God has declared certain activities to be good and others to be sinful, Christians can rightly call those activities what God calls them. Sleeping with someone else other than your spouse, lying, stealing, perverse speech, drunkenness, and so on, are all sins. Being faithful to your spouse, loving your neighbor, loving God, are all good.

Speaking of judging, do you know that one day you are going to stand before God to be judged for the things you've done in this life (Ecclesiastes 12:14; Revelation 20:11–15)? Would you like to make sure all your sins have been forgiven and washed away before that day?

"There is no neutral ground when it comes to the tolerance question. Everybody has a point of view she thinks is right, and everybody passes judgment at some point or another. The Christian gets pigeonholed as the judgmental one, but everyone else is judging, too, even people who consider themselves relativists."

–Greg Koukl

37. "Why do Christians hate homosexuals and say they are going to Hell?"

I know hundreds of Christians, and none of them have ever told me they hate homosexuals. Many Christians have friends or family members who identify as homosexuals or lesbians. And we love these people!

Do you assume that we hate them because we believe sexual activity between two people of the same sex is sinful?

We also believe the Bible condemns sexual activity between unmarried males and females (1 Corinthians 6:9; Hebrews 13:4). Does that mean we hate those people also? No. Friend, believing a particular *activity* is displeasing to God does not mean we hate the *persons* who engage in those activities. I have five kids at home and I view some of their activities unfavorably. And I even tell them occasionally, "What you're doing is sinful. That behavior is not pleasing to God." Does this mean I hate them? Of course not. I tell them that because I love them.

As for Hell, we all deserve to go there (Matthew 5:20–22). And the Bible makes it clear that anyone who turns away God's gracious offer of forgiveness will end up there. If a person says, "I don't want You God, I don't care what You say about how to live or what Jesus did for me on the cross," that person will have his way in the end. No God. No Heaven.

> "If you believe what you like in the gospels, and reject what you don't like, it is not the gospel you believe, but yourself."
> **–Augustine**

> "We are called to be the people of the truth, even when the truth is not popular and even when the truth is denied by the culture around us. Christians have found themselves in this position before, and we will again. God's truth has not changed. The holy Scriptures have not changed. The gospel of Jesus Christ has not changed. The church's mission has not changed. Jesus Christ is the same, yesterday, today and tomorrow."
> **–Albert Mohler**

38. "Belief in God is a crutch! Christians believe in God because they're weak and afraid of facing life and death on their own."

Oh, I like crutches. Have you ever had a sprained ankle or broken leg? Crutches are helpful in those kinds of situations, aren't they?

In a sense, God is like a crutch. He helps people who have been wounded and broken by sin to make it through this life and on into Heaven.

But, of course, you're free to hobble your way through this life without God's help. He's not going to force you to have a relationship with Him. The forgiveness, comfort, strength, joy, guidance, peace, and everlasting life He gives are for those who know Him and walk with Him.

I must warn you, though. If you reject God's gracious offer of forgiveness, you will stand before Him on the Day of Judgment and every sinful thing you said and did in this life is going to be brought to light and judged. You will be justly condemned and cast into Hell (Hebrews 10:31; Romans 2:5–9).

Friend, you don't want to end up there. Repent and place your faith in Jesus Christ today!

"Some say Christianity is just a crutch. But let's turn the question on its edge for a moment. Is atheism an emotional crutch, wishful thinking?...Perhaps atheists are rejecting God because they've had a bad relationship with their father.

Instead of inventing God, have atheists invented non-God?
Have they invented atheism to escape some of the frightening
implications of God's existence? Think about it."
–Greg Koukl

"Atheism provides a hiding place for those who do not
want to acknowledge and repent of their sins."
–Dinesh D'Souza

"I don't believe in Christianity because it makes me feel good
(often it doesn't), but for one reason: because it is true."
–Andy Bannister

39. "It's foolish to believe in things you can't see, like this God you speak of."

Can I ask you a couple questions? Have you ever seen your thoughts? But do they exist? Have you ever seen gravity? Do you believe gravity is real? When you see a painting, do you need to see the painter to conclude a painter exists? No.

So, some things that are invisible or currently out of view are actually real, aren't they? Well, the same is true with God. We don't need to see God to confidently conclude He exists.

What seems foolish to me is the popular alternative to believing in God—the belief that the entire space-time-matter-universe sprang into existence from what Richard Dawkins says was "literally nothing."[65] Then, sometime later, the non-living matter mysteriously came to life, split up into millions of little parts that then assembled themselves over millions of years into thousands of incredibly complex living creatures with bones, muscles, lungs, hearts, and brains. And how did that all happen? Atheists say by billions of *unseen* random macroevolutionary steps.

So, we *all* believe in the unseen. But which unseen scenario is more likely to be true? The molecular biologist Francis Crick, an atheist, and one of the two scientists who discovered DNA, "estimates the odds that intelligent life exists on the Earth as the result of non-directed chance to be around 1 in 10 to the two billionth power."[66] Friend, I wouldn't bet against God's existence with odds like that. It would be wiser to conclude God must exist and surrender your life to Him today.

"As Christians we accept one big miracle: God, and everything else makes sense. An atheist denies God and has to have a miracle for every other thing."
–John MacArthur

"It is absurd for the evolutionists to complain that it's unthinkable for an admittedly unthinkable God to make everything out of nothing and then pretend it is more thinkable that nothing should turn itself into anything." **–G. K. Chesterton**

....

65. Richard Dawkins, "Something from Nothing and the Magic of Reality–Part 2," http://www.youtube.com/watch?v=ygXDWOp2vgs.

66. Mike Licona, "Answering Lenny Flank's Article Against Intelligent Design," https://www.risenjesus.com/answering-lenny-flanks-article-against-intelligent-design.

"Just because something is unseen doesn't mean it's not real. There are many unseen realities that scientists use every day, such as the laws of logic, the laws of mathematics, the laws of nature, their minds, and so forth. And scientists infer from the effects they do see to causes they don't see. John Lennox observes, 'Postulating an unobserved Designer is no more unscientific than postulating unobserved macroevolutionary steps.'"

–Frank Turek

40. "The Bible is oppressive and harmful to women!"

Have you read the Bible or did you just pick up that line somewhere else? What passages in the Bible did you find most oppressive? Tell me about them.

Friend, I encourage you to reread the Bible. I've been studying the Bible for a long time, and it's clear to me that God loves and cherishes women. And millions of *women* who read the Bible every day have concluded the same thing.

They've understood that the Bible says men and women are *both* made in the image of God (Genesis 1:26–27) and are equally valuable and important to God (Galatians 3:28). They've read Paul's instructions for husbands to love their wives even as Jesus loves them and was willing to lay down His life on the cross for their sins (Ephesians 5:25). They've read the passages where men are told to do "nothing from selfishness" and to even consider women ("one another") to be more important than themselves (Philippians 2:3). They've read about the wonderful friendships Jesus had with women like Mary and Martha or where women like Ruth, Deborah, Priscilla and others are portrayed in a wonderful light. They've understood that the Bible condemns activities that hurt women, like physical and emotional abuse, adultery, abandoning one's wife, and rape.

My friend, if people would follow the teachings of the Bible more closely, the world would be a much better place for women.

41. "We look at ancient Greeks, with their gods on a mountaintop, throwing lightning bolts, and say 'They were so silly, so primitive and naïve. Not like our religion. We have burning bushes talking to people, and guys walking on water. We're so sophisticated.'"[67]

Have you read the Book of Exodus? Friend, it wasn't a bush talking to people; it was God speaking to Moses out of a burning bush. Is that not allowed? What's unreasonable about that? If you can talk, isn't it reasonable to assume that the One who created your mouth can talk? If a shipwrecked man can manage to start a fire to get the attention of a passing ship, can't God create a fire to get the attention of a man (Exodus 3:2)? And if God came to the Earth in the person of Jesus,

---

67. This objection was a popular meme on social media.

couldn't He perform miracles, like walking on water (Matthew 14:26)? Wouldn't you *expect* Him to do some miracles to validate who He was?

Atheists frequently say, "If God exists, He should do a miracle to prove He exists!" But when God came to the Earth and did miracles, people nailed Him to a wooden cross. And today, with their feet firmly planted on the Earth God created, breathing the air God made, they wag their God-fashioned-tongues insisting that acts of God (miracles) aren't possible. Oh the irony! *They* are a miracle, living in a miracle! What regret they will have when they stand before His throne on the Day of Judgment! Their "sophistication" in rejecting miracles is going to seem utterly foolish.

"If there is a God who can act, then there can be acts of God. The only way to show that miracles are impossible is to disprove the existence of God."
–Norman Geisler

42. "I believe in science! Most scientists are atheists. So, I find science and Christianity to be incompatible."

Christianity and science are certainly not incompatible. If they were, there wouldn't be any scientists today who are Christians. But there are a lot of scientists who are Christians. Dr. Jeffrey Russell, Professor of History at UC Santa Barbara, says, "about forty percent of professional natural scientists are practicing Christians, and many others are theists of other kinds. Fewer than thirty percent are atheists."[68] It's just not true that most scientists today are atheists.

Many of history's greatest scientists believed in God—Francis Bacon (1561–1626), Galileo (1564–1642), Kepler (1571–1630), Pascal (1623–62), Boyle (1627–91), Newton (1642–1727), Faraday (1791–1867), Babbage (1791–1871), Mendel (1822–84), Pasteur (1822–95), Kelvin (1824–1907), and Clerk Maxwell (1831–79), just to name a few.[69] It was often their confidence that God existed, that inspired their research and investigation. They expected to unearth laws in nature because they believed in a Lawgiver.[70]

You may be surprised to learn that the Bible revealed several details about the Earth and the universe long before scientists discovered them to be true. For example, the Biblical authors revealed that the universe had a beginning (Genesis 1:1), that the Earth is a round sphere (Job 26:10; Isaiah 40:22), that ocean water is the source of river water flowing into the ocean (Ecclesiastes 1:7; Job 36:27–28; Amos 9:6), that the stars are uncountable (Jeremiah 33:22), that the Sun travels on a circuit through the heavens (Psalm 19:6), that the amount of useable energy in the universe is decreasing (Psalm 102:25–27), that the Earth is completely unattached in space (Job 26:7), and that there are springs at the bottom of the ocean (Genesis 7:11; Job 38:16).

----

68. Jeffrey Burton Russell, *Exposing Myths About Christianity: A Guide to Answering 145 Viral Lies and Legends* (2012), 147.

69. For an excellent overview of these scientists and their faith in God, see Henry Morris, *Men of Science, Men of God: Great Scientists Who Believed the Bible.*

70. John Lennox, *God's Undertaker: Has Science Buried God?* (2009), 21.

Would you be willing to watch a video that examines these kinds of details in the Bible?[71] Either way, you can be confident that Christianity and science are compatible.

"Holy Scripture could never lie or err...its decrees are of absolute and inviolable truth."
–Galileo Galilei

"Far from belief in God hindering science, it was the motor that drove it. Isaac Newton, when he discovered the law of gravitation, did not make the common mistake of saying: 'now I have a law of gravity, I don't need God'. Instead, he wrote Principia Mathematica, *the most famous book in the history of science, expressing the hope that it would persuade the thinking man to believe in a Creator."*
–John Lennox

"The rule that science is the only way to know something is itself unscientific; it cannot be tested. So the claim that only science can demonstrate truth actually flunks its own test, since it cannot validate itself!"
–Gary Habermas

71. I like to give people my DVD, *The Bible's Scientific Accuracy & Foresight* (2018), available at AlwaysBeReady.com.

43. "A talking snake in the Garden of Eden (Genesis 3)? How do you believe this stuff?"

The Bible was not referring to an ordinary snake speaking. Scripture reveals that the serpent was actually Satan (Revelation 12:9, 20:2), an angel who had rejected God and was intent on leading the first humans to join the rebellion. And he's still deceiving people today.

Do you think he's ever deceived you? Mind if I ask you a question? Do you think inorganic, non-living matter like hydrogen or rocks would ever be able to talk? No. Sounds more absurd than a snake speaking, doesn't it? But millions of people today believe that a long time ago, inorganic, non-living material sprang into existence from what Richard Dawkins calls "literally nothing."[72] Then a very long time after that, the matter came to life, busted into all kinds of living parts, machinery, and information that somehow attached themselves to each other to form different organisms. Then these organisms slowly evolved into male and female human bodies with 206 bones,[73] about 700 muscles,[74] and hearts that beat more than 100,000 times a day pumping blood through 60,000 miles of veins, arteries and capillaries in the human body.[75] Then, these

....

72. Richard Dawkins, "Something from Nothing and the Magic of Reality–Part 2," http://www.youtube.com/watch?v=ygXDWOp2vgs.

73. Donald Rizzo, *Fundamentals of Anatomy and Physiology* (2016), 175.

74. Innerbody, "Muscular System," http://www.innerbody.com/image/musfov.html.

75. Arkansas Heart Hospital, "Amazing Heart Facts," https://www.arheart.com/heart-health/amazing-heart-facts.

humans, having developed eyes, mouths, tongues, lungs, ears, and brains, were able to create and speak a variety of different languages.

Friend, can you understand why some very intelligent people find that evolutionary tale a thousand times harder to believe than an angel speaking? Why *do* so many people believe the tale? Satan, who deceived Eve in the Garden, is still at work deceiving people today (John 8:44; 2 Corinthians 4:4).

"In their case, the god of this age [Satan] has blinded the minds of the unbelievers to keep them from seeing the light of the gospel of the glory of Christ, who is the image of God."
–**Paul** (2 Corinthians 4:4)

"I have noticed that whenever a person gives up his belief in the Word of God because it requires that he should believe a good deal, his unbelief requires him to believe a great deal more. If there be any difficulties in the faith of Christ, they are not one-tenth as great as the absurdities in any system of unbelief which seeks to take its place."
–**Charles Spurgeon**

44. "All religions basically teach the same thing. If a person is sincere, it's all going to be okay in the end."

How did you come to that conclusion? Have you studied the teachings of the world's religions? What doctrines did you find to be the same?

Friend, there are some superficial similarities with some of them. But when you look at the foundational core teachings of the religions, you discover that they contradict one another left and right on a lot of big questions. For example, who is God? What is he, she, or it like? How and why do humans exist? Why is there evil and suffering in the world? What happens to a person after he dies? So, the religions of the world certainly don't all "teach the same thing." And because that is the case, they certainly cannot all be true.

One of the reasons Christians have put their faith in Jesus is because He did something no other founder of a religion has ever done. He backed up His claims by doing things only God can do. He opened the eyes of the blind (Mark 10:52). He brought the dead back to life (John 11:44). He healed crippled people with a word (Matthew 15:30). He rose from the grave three days after He was put to death (Luke 24:6).

In addition to His miracles, He fulfilled dozens of Old Testament prophecies that were written down centuries before He was born (e.g., Micah 5:2, Isaiah 35:5–6, Psalm 22:16–18; Isaiah 53; Daniel 9:24–26; Psalm 16:10). And He lived a sinless life (2 Corinthians 5:21)! Jesus is someone you can trust.

Friend, things can turn out far better for you than "okay in the end." If you'll place your faith in Jesus to save your soul, there will be no end. He offers people the free gift of everlasting life in His kingdom (John 3:16)! So, I urge you to place your faith in Him today.

"Every religion in the world except one says you must work your way to God. Only Biblical Christianity says God has worked His way to you."
–Ed Hindson

"All religions and philosophies say, 'This is the way.' Only Jesus says, 'I am the Way.'"
–Tim Keller

"There are only two kinds of religion in the world... They all say, "Do, do, do." Only Christianity says, "Done." Christ has done it all."
–J. Vernon McGee

"Unsophisticated religious pluralism responds to the religious diversity of mankind by saying, "Well, they are all true! All of the world's religions are basically saying the same thing." This view, which you very often find on the lips of college sophomores and laypeople, just evinces, frankly, tremendous ignorance of the teachings of the world's great religions. Anybody who has studied even a little bit of comparative religion knows that the worldviews that are propounded by these different religions are diametrically opposed to each other. Therefore, they cannot all be true."
–William Lane Craig

45. "Christians worship the same God as Muslims!"

Why do you think that? What are some of the *similarities* between the God revealed in the Bible and the god spoken of in the Quran? Do you know there are some major *differences* between Yahweh and Allah?

For example, Muhammad said his god, Allah, was not triune in nature[76]—Father, Son, and Holy Spirit—as plainly revealed in the Bible.[77]

Muhammad condemned the belief that Jesus is God.[78] Of course, the Bible indicates Jesus was and is God (John 1:1, 20:28; Titus 2:13; 2 Peter 1:1).

Muhammad said Jesus was never put to death on a cross,[79] something of course the Bible (Matthew 27:35), Flavius Josephus, and others say occurred.[80]

Muhammad repeatedly said Allah does not love sinners.[81] The God of the Bible loves the whole world (John 3:16; Romans 5:8).

....

76. Quran 4:171

77. See Ron Rhodes's excellent defense of the Biblical doctrine of the Trinity, "The Trinity: A Case Study in Implicit Truth," http://www.equip.org/articles/the-trinity-a-case-study-in-implicit-truth. Also see Matt Slick's helpful "Trinity Chart," https://carm.org/trinity.

78. Quran 112:1–4, 4:48, 171.

79. Quran 4:157

80. Josephus, *Antiquities of the Jews*, Book 18, Chapter 3:3; Cornelius Tacitus, *Annals*, 15.44.

81. Here are a few examples from the Quran: "Allah does not love any ungrateful sinner" (2:276); "Surely Allah does not love the unbelievers" (3:32); "Surely Allah does not love him who is proud" (4:36); "Allah does not love the mischief-makers" (5:64); "Surely He does not love the extravagant" (6:14).

Muhammad said a person's good works must outweigh his bad works if he hopes to make it to Paradise.[82] The Bible says everlasting life is a "free gift" to those who place their faith in Jesus (Romans 6:23, 10:9–13).

Muhammad taught that the only way to be assured of entry to Paradise, was to die in jihad for Allah.[83] But the Bible says that Jesus, God in the flesh, died for us (Romans 5:6–8).

Friend, Christians do not worship the god that Muhammad invented 600 years after Jesus was born. We worship the true God who revealed Himself to Abraham 2700 years earlier.[84]

46. "That's just your interpretation of the Bible!"

Do you say that because you don't *like* my interpretation, or because you think I'm *mistaken* about my interpretation? Do you have a better interpretation? If I pull up the passage in my Bible app, would you be willing to read the verse and tell me what *you* think it means?

The Bible is quite clear on most matters. I think a lot of people reject the Bible, not because it's *difficult* to understand, but because they understand what it says and just don't *like* it.

....

82. Quran 23:102–3 says, "Then those whose balance (of good deeds) is heavy, they will attain salvation: But those whose balance is light, will be those who have lost their souls, in Hell will they abide." Quran 18:107 says, "As to those who believe and work righteous deeds, they have, for their entertainment, the Gardens of Paradise... And whoever hopeth for the meeting with his Lord, let him do righteous work."

83. Quran 2:154, 3:157, 169–170.

84. God initiated a covenant with Abraham around 2090 BC (Genesis 12). Muhammad was allegedly visited by the angel Gabriel for the first time 2700 years later in AD 610.

It convicts them of their drunkenness, fornication, adultery, pride, and so on. And they don't like that (John 7:7). They want to live their lives free from any moral constraints (John 3:19). They want to ease their troubled consciences. And so, they come up with excuses like, "The Bible was written by fallible men!" or "The Bible is just an ancient collection of legends."

Sadly, they have misunderstood the intent of God's instructions. They weren't given to rob us of joy or pleasure. God's instructions in the Bible were given because He loves us. He designed us. He knows what's best for us. And He desires that we know and experience joy (Philippians 4:4; 1 Timothy 6:17), peace (John 14:27), and abundant life (John 10:10).

"The thief comes only to steal and kill and destroy; I came that they may have life, and have it abundantly."
–Jesus (John 10:10)

"When a person refuses to come to Christ it is never just because of lack of evidence or because of intellectual difficulties: at root, he refuses to come because he willingly ignores and rejects the drawing of God's Spirit on his heart. No one in the final analysis really fails to become a Christian because of lack of arguments; he fails to become a Christian because he loves darkness rather than light and wants nothing to do with God."
–William Lane Craig

"Men loved the darkness rather than the Light, for their deeds were evil"
–Jesus (John 3:19)

47. "I will never be happy in Heaven if my friends and family end up in Hell."

Well, if you're concerned about being happy, you certainly don't want to end up in Hell. There won't be *any* happiness there! The Bible says there is going to be weeping and wailing in Hell (Matthew 8:12, 13:42, 25:30).

Friend, it's hard to know with certainty this side of death where your friends or family members will spend eternity. Some of those who already died may have placed their faith in Jesus before it was too late. But even if they rejected God's offer of forgiveness and everlasting life, that doesn't mean you should also.

I can assure you of this—people are going to be happy in Heaven! The Bible says there is "fullness of joy" there (Psalm 16:11). It also says in Heaven there won't be any mourning, crying, or pain (Revelation 21:4). None. Ever! So, put your faith in Jesus today, look forward to going to Heaven, and allow God to use you while there's still time to share the gospel with your loved ones who are still alive.

48. "You should stop trying to force your beliefs on people!"

When Jesus died on the cross for our sins and then rose from the grave three days later, He told His followers to share the good news with the whole world. That's all I'm doing. I'm not trying to *force* anyone to believe. I'm explaining God's gracious offer of forgiveness and everlasting life to people. It's news that's too good to keep to myself.

If someone had the cure for a deadly disease and kept it to himself, people would consider it a crime. Well the good news about Jesus is better than the cure for the deadliest disease. It's the cure for sin and death!

How about you? Who is Jesus to you? Do you believe in Heaven and Hell? When you die, where will you go? Why do you think that? If what you believe is wrong, would you want to know?

49. "I'm a good person. Surely, God is not going to send good people to Hell!"

May I ask you a few questions? Over the course of your life, how many lies do you think you've told? Those are sins (Exodus 20:16). Have you ever stolen something? (Exodus 20:15). Have you had sexual intercourse with someone you weren't married to? That's called fornication or adultery in the Bible, and those are sins (1 Corinthians 6:9; Exodus 20:14). Have you hungered after (coveted) something that didn't belong to you? (Exodus 20:17). Have you ever replaced a vulgar foul word with the name of Jesus? (Exodus 20:7). Have you ever disobeyed or dishonored your parents? (Exodus 20:12). Have you ever been drunk? (Ephesians 5:18).

Friend, like me, you need God's forgiveness! And we've only considered a handful of God's commandments. Your good deeds don't cancel out any of your previous bad deeds. If you reject God's offer of forgiveness, reconciliation, and salvation, you are going to be judged for those sins (Ecclesiastes 12:14; Matthew 12:36), justly condemned, and end up in Hell (Romans 2:5; Revelation 20:15). The choice is up to you.

> *"We know that a person is not justified by works of the law but through faith in Jesus Christ... by works of the law no one will be justified."*
> **–Paul** (Galatians 2:16)

> *"The puzzling question is not, 'Why would God send good people to Hell?', but rather 'Why would a just God allow bad people into Heaven?'"*
> **–Alan Sheldon**

> *"I believe that the damned are, in one sense, successful rebels to the end; that the doors of Hell are locked on the inside."*
> **–C. S. Lewis**

50. "You Christians are so narrow-minded! Insisting that a person has to have a relationship with Jesus to go to Heaven is preposterous!"

Well, that is what the Bible teaches (John 14:6; Acts 4:12; 1 Timothy 2:5). Do you think the Bible is mistaken? How do *you* think a person gets to Heaven? How did you come to that conclusion? What evidence is there for that belief?

God's offer of forgiveness might sound preposterous and narrow to you, but His offer is actually very broad and gracious. None of us deserve to go to Heaven. We all deserve judgment and death. But amazingly, Jesus told His disciples to take the good news about forgiveness of sins and share it "even to the remotest part of the Earth" (Luke 24:47; Acts 1:8). Isn't that incredible? No one—even the guiltiest of sinners—is excluded from His offer. Anyone can place their faith in Jesus and be forgiven and granted "everlasting life" (John 3:16; Romans 10:13).

Would you agree with me that the only person who can forgive an offender and restore him to a right relationship with himself is the one who has been injured or sinned against?

The reason Jesus is the only one who can forgive our sins is because He's God. He's the one we've sinned against. We can't cry out to deities that deceitful men invented and expect them to save us. We need to be reconciled to the God who really exists, Jesus. And thankfully, we can be, because of His death on the cross for our sins. Would you like God to forgive you for your sins? You can call out to God right now. Pray something like this:

God, thank You for loving me. I'm so sorry for my sins. I want to turn away from them. I renounce them! I believe Jesus died on the cross for my sins. So, please forgive me. Wash away my sins. I trust in Jesus Christ to save me. Come into my life. Be my Lord and Savior and make me into the person You want me to be. Amen!

The Bible says, "Whoever calls upon the name of the Lord will be saved" (Romans 10:13). So, if you have placed your faith in Jesus, God has forgiven you of your sins. The apostle John said, "These things I have written to you who believe in the name of the Son of God, so that you may know that you have eternal life" (1 John 5:13). Now begins an exciting new journey, walking with God.

To grow in your relationship with God...

A. Begin reading through the New Testament.

Get a good "study Bible." I recommend the *ESV Study Bible* or *The NKJV Study Bible*. These have helpful notes in them that will explain the historical context, meaning of passages, etc.

B. Start talking (praying) to God.

He loves you and wants to have a relationship with you. You can talk to Him about anything. "The prayer of the upright is His delight" (Prov. 15:8).

C. Get connected to a conservative Bible-believing church where the Bible is trusted and studied in its entirety.

Check out the church's "Doctrinal Statement" or "Beliefs" on their website. If they don't clearly lay out their beliefs, stay away. The church should hold to doctrines similar to alwaysbeready. com/abr-beliefs. These are held widely by Christian churches all over the world. If the church has a new believer's class, sign up to attend. Please steer clear of Mormon ("Latter Day Saints") and Jehovah's Witnesses churches. These groups claim to be Christian, but they espouse many unbiblical doctrines.

D. Get connected with other Christians.

It's important to find other Christians who can encourage you and be a blessing to you in your new relationship with Jesus. If you have friends or family members who are Christians, let them know of the decision you've made. They will rejoice and pray for you.

Q&A with Charlie Campbell

Where do you live? San Diego, California.

Are you married? Yes. And my wife and I have five wonderful kids (see p. 93).

Where did you and your wife meet? A Bible study for young adults in Newport Beach, CA. Wednesday evening, March 26, 1997. I was convinced after our first conversation that I had met the girl I wanted to marry.

What do you do for work? I write books and speak at churches and conferences on topics related to the defense of the Christian faith.

How long have you been doing that? Full-time since 2005.

What did you do before that? I taught at the Calvary Chapel Bible College in Murrieta, California, and the School of Ministry at Calvary Vista, CA, where I worked from 1997–2005.

What classes did you teach? Apologetics, world religions and cults, systematic theology, eschatology, church history, hermeneutics, homiletics, and evangelism.

What led you to become interested in apologetics? Reading a couple of good apologetics books back in 1990 led me to believe in God and trust the Bible. I've been interested in apologetics ever since.

You've been traveling since 2005 speaking at churches and conferences. How did that come about? The itinerant ministry wasn't something I was planning on or saw coming. I was teaching apologetics classes and word started spreading to pastors that there was a guy who could come to their church and encourage people regarding the reliability of the Bible, evidence for God, and so on. In 2005, the invitations to come and speak started coming in so frequently that my wife and I prayerfully decided that God was opening a door for me to minister full-time in that manner.

What advice would you give to someone who wants to be better able to "contend for the faith"? First, study the Bible. Many of the attacks on the faith can be countered by having a better grasp on the Bible. Second, supplement your study with good apologetics articles, books, and videos. Our website, AlwaysBeReady.com, is brimming with these kinds of resources. So that's a good place to start.

What Christian apologist has influenced you the most? Norman Geisler.

If you could get lunch with any person in the Bible, other than Jesus, who would it be? Paul.

Lunch with anyone *outside* the Bible? Charles Spurgeon.

Favorite foods? Mexican. Thai. Indian.

Three things people are surprised to find out about you? I was petrified of public speaking before I became a Christian. I have five kids. I play guitar and bass.

Where are some of your favorite places you've visited? My top ten would be Israel, Kauai, Costa Rica, Oregon, Yosemite, Scotland, Austria, Lake Tahoe, Banff, and Mammoth.

Favorite sports teams? San Diego Padres and LA Chargers.

What do you like to do for fun? I love to hike and explore God's creation with my wife and kids. Surf. Snowboard. Ride my beach cruiser, play basketball and ping-pong with my kids.

What three things would you bring to a deserted island? My Bible, acoustic guitar, and a camera.

What are you most grateful for? God. Forgiveness of my sins. Everlasting life. The Bible. Family. Friends. Good health. Opportunities to speak at churches.

OTHER BOOKS BY CHARLIE CAMPBELL

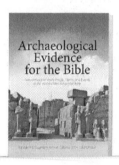
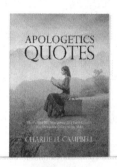

Archaeological Evidence for the Bible (Updated 2020 Edition!)

———————

Learn about dozens of archaeological discoveries that have verified people, places, and events in the Bible. Includes 100+ color photographs.

Apologetics Quotes

———————

500 of the best quotes by leading defenders of the Christian faith:

- Norman Geisler
- Lee Strobel
- Ravi Zacharias
- Josh McDowell
- C. S. Lewis
- Ron Rhodes
- William Craig
- John MacArthur
- and more

Teaching & Preaching God's Word

———————

Has God called you to preach His Word? If so, you'll love this book. In 78 concise chapters, Charlie shares several ideas, exhortations, and words of encouragement on sermon preparation and preaching.

AMAZINGLY...

this little USB flash drive contains Charlie Campbell's entire library of videos (mp4s) and audio lectures (mp3s) on a wide range of apologetic issues. Just plug it into the USB port on your television or computer and begin watching or listening. You can also transfer the files to your iPad, iPhone, or other tablet (simple directions included). These videos and lectures will strengthen your faith in God and the Bible and equip you to answer atheists, skeptics, Muslims, Mormons, Jehovah's Witnesses, Hindus, Buddhists, New Agers, and others. Free shipping in the USA.

Questions? Email us at: **abr@alwaysbeready.com**.

WANT TO CONTINUE LEARNING? TAKE CHARLIE'S ONLINE APOLOGETICS COURSE.

If you enjoyed this book, you'll love Charlie Campbell's online apologetics course. All classes are on-demand videos that stream right to your device any time of day. Classes include: "Evidence for God," "Answering Atheists' Objections to God and the Bible," "Why Does God Allow Evil and Suffering?" and more! Enroll today at:

AlwaysBeReady.Teachable.com
Oh, and no homework or tests — just fun times of learning!

Index

99

Characteristics of a God-Glorifying Ambassador of Jesus Christ

1. Loving.

"Watch, stand fast in the faith, be brave, be strong. Let all that you do be done with love." (1 Corinthians 16:13–14)

2. Ready, but gentle and respectful.

"Always be ready to give a defense to everyone who asks you a reason for the hope that is in you, yet do it with gentleness and respect..." (1 Peter 3:15)

3. Gracious.

"Let your speech always be with grace, seasoned with salt..." (Colossians 4:6)

4. Patient.

"And a servant of the Lord must not quarrel but be gentle to all, able to teach, patient, in humility correcting those who are in opposition..." (2 Timothy 2:24–26)

5. Humble.

"So then neither the one who plants nor the one who waters is anything, but God who causes the growth." (1 Corinthians 3:7)

6. Discerning.

"Do not give what is holy to the dogs; nor cast your pearls before swine, lest they trample them under their feet, and turn and tear you in pieces." (Matthew 7:6)

7. Obedient to Jesus's Great Commission.

"Go therefore and make disciples of all the nations, baptizing them in the name of the Father and of the Son and of the Holy Spirit, teaching them to observe all things that I have commanded you; and lo, I am with you always, even to the end of the age. Amen." (Matthew 28:19–20)

Made in the USA
Coppell, TX
14 December 2022

89261480R00059